# PSALMS OF THE HEART

Other books by
**George Sweeting**

*Catch the Spirit of Love*

*How to Begin the Christian Life*

*How to Discover the Will of God*

*Your Future*

*Special Sermons*

*Acts of God*

# PSALMS OF THE HEART

## GEORGE SWEETING

This book is designed for both enjoyable reading
and group study. For study purposes, obtain a leader's guide
with visual aids (Victor Multiuse Transparency Masters) from your
local bookstore or from the publisher.

## VICTOR BOOKS ®

A DIVISION OF SCRIPTURE PRESS PUBLICATIONS INC.
USA CANADA ENGLAND

Recommended Dewey Decimal Classification: 223.2
Suggested Subject Headings: BIBLE, O.T. PSALMS

Library of Congress Catalog Card Number: 87-62488
ISBN: 0-89693-435-7

# CONTENTS

# Contents

# INTRODUCTION

We live in a generation that is dazzled by image. There are people who make great sums of money as image-makers. Not the ancient kind, but the kind where people and products are skillfully packaged in a way that is designed to impress. It is what's on the outside that counts—externals! The quality of a product or the character of a person is assumed to be less important.

Television highlights this trend. Its personalities are almost flawless. The studio, the camera, and the editors work their tricks to hide all the blemishes. It is no secret that our media age caters to the beautiful people in every field. It is difficult to imagine a person like the rotund William Howard Taft, our twenty-seventh President, being elected today, mainly because of the unathletic size and shape of his body.

In direct contrast to this modern approach, the Bible says that "the Lord seeth not as man seeth, for man looketh on the outward appearance, but the Lord looketh on the heart" (1 Sam. 16:7, KJV). The Bible—and particularly the Psalms—show that the real and final test of a person's life is the attitude of his heart toward God and man.

The Psalms penetrate our cosmetic special effects and begin a work of confronting, convicting, and comforting the human spirit. In a sense, the Psalms of the Bible are a general hospital of the soul where we might each select medicine for our diseases. They are honest prayers which help us articulate praise and complaint before the living God.

Not long ago, I had a Christian friend who was struck by tragedy. In an hour of shock and grief, when no ordinary words were appropriate, his simple request was, "Read me the Psalms!"

Too many Christians ignore the Psalms. We forget that they have been a prayer book for Christians and Jews for centuries.

7

We forget that they played a central part in Old Testament temple worship. We forget how prominent they were in the worship of the early church. And we forget that they served as models for our earliest Christian hymns.

In this book, I have chosen to write about *my favorite psalms*. Some of them you will recognize. Others may be new to you. But all of them will plunge beneath the surface, bringing spiritual lessons to the heart about the basics of life.

*Dedicated to quality friends*

Bob and Betsy Wiker

Louis and Jane Myre

Emily Keenan

George and Ruth Mak

# CHAPTER ONE

# GOD'S BLUEPRINT FOR SUCCESS

## PSALM 1

Recently, *Esquire* magazine gave over 500 lines to the subject of success in an article titled "The Best of the New Generation." It zeroed in on successful people under age forty who are changing America.

The criteria for being a success, according to *Esquire*, included a career of genuine value, personal initiative, risk-taking, an enthusiastic "can-do" attitude, creative impulse, strong will-power, and persistence. These traits, according to the author, mark the heroes of our generation.

*Esquire* focused exclusively on professional excellence, with public achievement and belief in oneself listed as chief values. *Esquire* chose to ignore qualities like personal morality, charac-ter, and religious commitment. Alarmingly, these characteris-tics were considered irrelevant to public life.

The definition of success in Psalm 1 is different from the criteria of *Esquire* magazine. The psalmist believed that spiritual commitment and personal morality of an individual have every-thing to do with "*real success.*" In Psalm 1 he defines success in terms of "character" rather than vocational skill.

With contrasting simplicity, Psalm 1 talks about two kinds of people: the blessed and the wicked.

## 1. THE BLESSED PERSON (Psalm 1:1-3)

Psalm 1 speaks of the blessed man (verses 1-3):

> Blessed is the man
>> Who walks not in the counsel of the ungodly,
>> Nor stands in the path of sinners,
>> Nor sits in the seat of the scornful;
> But his delight is in the Law of the Lord,
>> And in His Law he meditates day and night.
> He shall be like a tree
>> Planted by the rivers of water,
>> That brings forth its fruit in its season,
>> Whose leaf also shall not wither;
> And whatever he does shall prosper.

Two pictures portray this successful person: his "way" and his comparison to a healthy tree. The successful person aims to please God. He avoids the ways of evil. The blessed person loves God and walks in His ways. He has a genuine thirst to know God. The direction of his life is not self-righteousness, but God's righteousness. He longs after God.

Self-righteousness is offensive. The Bible never commends it. But the day we frown on *true righteousness* is the day we stand against God's way. Some American journalists now use the word *righteousness* in the same derogatory way they once used the word *self-righteousness*. May God help the society that confuses the two!

The godly person affirms the righteousness of God. His success comes because he wisely follows the way of God Almighty.

What do we mean by the word *blessed*? Kenneth Taylor in *The Living Bible* renders it, "Happy are those" (Matt. 5:6-10).

The person is blessed because he knows life as God meant it to be lived.

The Old Testament often describes blessing in physical terms. The blessed person has health, security, abundance, and lots of children. However, there are times when a blessed person's reward does not come until the future. Remember Job? He knew pain and heartache. But Job was also positive that he was walking in the way of the Lord. He knew that the future would reward him.

The New Testament pictures quite similar conditions to those of Psalm 1. In the Sermon on the Mount, Jesus said, "Blessed are those who mourn," and "Blessed are those who are persecuted . . . , for theirs is the kingdom of heaven" (Matt. 5:4, 10).

As we see the Bible as a whole, "blessedness" means "success." It can be physical success but it is usually spiritual. It can be present but it is often future.

Psalm 1 describes a series of conditions for success. Negatively, success comes *from avoiding evil*. When we become believers in Christ, we renounce evil. Likewise, the successful Christian steers clear of the evil ways of the wicked. He treats evil like a contagious deadly poison. At one time, poisonous liquids carried the symbol of a skull and crossbones. This was a blunt reminder that drinking them could be fatal. So it is with evil.

Psalm 1:1 speaks of three levels of openness to evil: thinking—when we *walk in its counsel*; behaving—when we stand in its path; and totally identifying—when we sit in the seat of the scorner. The blessed person avoids all three levels. To open the mind to ungodly counsel gradually transforms character. It is like Dr. Jekyll taking his first sip of the deadly potion. After the liquid touches his bloodstream, he turns into the monstrous Mr. Hyde.

First, verse 1 says that the blessed person "walks not in the counsel of the ungodly." Rather, he guards his mind against ungodly counsel. Our mind is the first wall of defense against sin. We must lock its doors to this wicked power if we are to succeed.

Did you know that *what your mind feeds on is important?* If you feed on mental junk food, you will live a junky life. If your diet is soap operas, gossip magazines, sensual novels, and/or questionable movies, then you will begin to live by these values.

Second, verse 1 reminds us that the blessed man does not "stand in the path of sinners." In other words, he does not behave as they do. Our lifestyles should announce that we are traveling in another direction. The righteous way is not just for Sunday strolls: it is a path for the rush hours Monday through Friday.

Third, verse 1 says that the blessed man does not "sit in the seat of the scornful." Sitting implies total identification. Scoffers are proud people. To sit with the proud implies a complete acceptance of their idolatrous points of view.

By contrast, the blessed man is wise. He will not even consider the evil way. He knows that even looking on evil can be dangerous. It can break down our defenses. Its powers cause us to forget its immediate danger. As Alexander Pope said, "When we see vice, first we are repulsed. Then we endure it. Then we pity it. Then we embrace it."

Beware of fascination with sin, as the psalmist says: evil casts its spell if we allow it in our door. The blessed man knows that it must be avoided. To consider it is to be enticed by it. And if enticed, we may suffer the same fate as those in the ancient myth who looked upon Medusa's head, and their hearts turned to stone.

The path to blessedness is not only negative: it also has a positive side. Success comes from choosing what is good. Verse 2 says that the blessed man's *"delight* is in the Law of the Lord, and in His Law he meditates day and night."

What do we mean by the Law? For the psalmist, it was the Books of Moses. In verse 2, the psalmist merely repeats Moses' charge to Joshua:

> This Book of the Law shall not depart from your mouth, but you shall meditate in it day and night, that you may observe to do according to all that is written in it. For then you will make your way prosperous, and then you will have good success (Josh. 1:8).

More than anything else, Moses wanted Joshua to be successful! So he instructed him to choose and cling to the revealed will of God as found in the Law of God.

For Christians, God's revealed will includes not only the Old Testament, but also the New Testament. Today we accept God's Law as His entire Word. So the positive road to success for Christians is to delight and meditate in God's Word.

How do we delight in His Word? We fill our minds with it and read it carefully. We soak our thoughts in it daily just like taking a long, hot bath. We let its heat open the pores of our soul and have its cleansing, soothing, reviving effect.

How do we meditate on God's Law? For the Hebrew, meditation meant memorizing it, reciting it, and testing it. We take it in and let it have a permanent place in our thoughts. We repeat it until it becomes a part of us. Then we live it. When we read its instruction, we obey it so that our way becomes God's way.

The world we live in has little time for this type of meditation. It wants action! Its slogans betray its shallowness: "Make it!"/"Go all the way!"/"Grab for all the gusto!" Its chief virtue is willpower.

The psalmist begs to disagree. He questions the so-called success of modern achievement. He views action without solid foundation as a dead-end street. It is wheel-spinning. It covers as much ground as a merry-go-round. And it has no redeeming value for individual souls.

For the psalmist, the person who aims at heaven and God's righteousness will get the earth thrown in. But the person who aims only at earth, gets neither heaven nor earth.

Consider the comparison the psalmist pictures in verse 3. He portrays the blessed man *as a tree* firmly planted by streams of water.

If you have ever planted trees, you know how most of them flourish where there is an abundance of water. Not long ago I planted a small willow tree in our back yard, and discovered its need for plenty of water. The secret of getting a willow to grow is to put it in the dampest part of your yard. If water gathers after a rain in a particular low spot, plant it there. If you live on a lake or near a creek, plant it there. Its growth is amazing when it gets adequate water.

The tree in Psalm 1 was planted by streams of water. It had plenty of water and minerals at its disposal. Trees like this are successful and bear lots of fruit.

So it is with men and women who drink deeply from God's Word. They shoot up into strong, sturdy Christians. They are rooted and stand firm. They bear abundant fruit.

But notice that the tree of Psalm 1 is subject to the seasons. The promise refers not to an absence of seasons but to an absence of drought. So it is with righteous people. They are subject to the seasons of life. They go through many winters. Yet the Lord sustains them from withering with living water. He gives them the Saviour, His Son, who said:

> Whoever drinks of the water that I shall give him
> will never thirst; but the water that I shall give him
> will become in him a fountain of water springing up
> to everlasting life (John 4:14).

This verse in John applies to the blessed, successful person of Psalm 1.

## 2. THE WICKED PERSON (Psalm 1:4-6)

After richly describing the success of the righteous, verse 4 declares, "The ungodly are *not so*, but are like the chaff which the wind drives away." The ungodly person goes in the exact opposite direction of the godly person. The righteous press toward the shining light of the city of God. The wicked run toward the darkness of the city of man.

In Daniel 6:10 we read that Daniel opened his windows toward Jerusalem. His gaze was on the holy city of God. His heart was set on worship in God's temple. On the other hand, in Genesis 13:12 we find that Lot pitched his tent toward Sodom. He was fascinated with that wicked city. When his wife hesitated and turned to look on Sodom in their flight from God's wrath, she became a pillar of salt. The evil of Sodom had finally transformed her heart.

When we think of wickedness, we tend to think too vividly. Orgies, drunkenness, and murder come to mind. However, the Bible defines wickedness as a condition of the heart. If a person gives his heart over to sin, he becomes hardened and begins to take on the features of evil.

Wickedness comes in different clothing. It can wear a three-piece suit. It can attend church once a week. It can lead a normal, civilized life.

The primary characteristic of wicked people is that they are *lost to themselves*. They shut God out and go their own way. They need not be theoretical atheists; they may be practical atheists—people who claim to believe in God but fail to live as if they know Him. They delight, not in His Law, but in themselves.

It should not surprise us that Psalm 1 compares the ungodly person to chaff. Remember the old-time farmer—the farmer who did things by hand? First, he thrashed the wheat—he separated the kernel from the husk. Then with a winnowing fork, he tossed it all up into the air. At that point, the wind did its work. It blew the fragments of chaff away. Only the usable grain remained.

The wicked often appear to be successful. They appear to be

heavyweights but they are midgets. But when they are tossed by the winds of adversity, they blow away. They are hopelessly driven by the external pressures of life. They are lightweights—hollow men and women. Before the wind and fire of God's judgment, they cannot stand.

Psalm 1 would not be complete without verses 5 and 6. Just as there are two kinds of people, so there are two destinations. The blessed person and the wicked person each have a destiny. Verses 5 and 6 read:

> Therefore the ungodly will not stand
>    in the judgment,
> Nor sinners in the congregation of the righteous.
> For the Lord knows the way of the righteous,
> But the way of the ungodly will perish.

There are only two ways to spend eternity—with or without God. Two places—heaven or hell.

The one constant feature of Psalm 1 is the fact of judgment. At some future day, all people, both righteous and wicked, will face God and give account of their lives.

Then comes a parting of ways. In no uncertain terms, the psalmist says that the wicked do not stand a chance. They persistently stand in defiance of God. They have chosen the way of destruction. In judgment, their desire to be without God will be granted. They will be treated like chaff.

The righteous, on the other hand, will join with the assembly of God's people. Verse 6 reads, "For the Lord knows the way of the righteous." He knows it because it is His way. He sent His Son to pioneer that way, to make men and women righteous, and to call them to follow Him. That way leads to eternal life. In Matthew 3, John the Baptist throws light on this judgment described in Psalm 1:

> His winnowing fan is in His hand, and He will thor-

oughly purge His threshing floor, and gather His wheat into the barn; but He will burn up the chaff with unquenchable fire (verse 12).

The psalmist pictures Jesus Christ as the Judge who shovels and tosses the threshed grain against the wind. Jesus will destroy the chaff.

These are sobering words. This is not a meek and mild Jesus. This is Jesus, the holy, righteous Son of God. He came into the world in order that we might not perish, but have everlasting life. And as many as receive Him, to them He gives the power to become children of God. Those who reject Him are literally banished from His presence forever.

Does your life resemble a tree planted, rooted, fruitful, and steadfast? Or are you blown about like straw which cannot endure the ultimate whirlwind of judgment?

Only *one kind of success* really counts. That is eternal success. That success can be yours as you decide to follow God's blueprint.

### REMEMBER

In Psalm 1, success is primarily a matter of character rather than vocational skill.

The blessed man loves God and walks in His path. He craves after God.

"When we see vice, first we are repulsed. Then we endure it. Then we pity it. Then we embrace it," declared Alexander Pope.

The positive road to success for Christians is to delight and meditate in God's Word.

For the psalmist, the man who aims at heaven and God's righteousness will get the earth thrown in. But the man who aims only at earth gets neither heaven nor earth.

According to the Bible, wickedness is primarily a condition of the heart.

# CHAPTER TWO

# GOD'S STANDARD
# OF EXCELLENCE

## PSALM 8

I t was baffling! *Time* magazine carried this quote from Soviet Premier Gorbachev: "Surely God on High has not refused to give us enough wisdom to bring improvement between the two great nations of the earth."

Imagine a Marxist premier referring to God in the press! Their government is officially atheistic. They actively oppress religion. The quote appears to be propaganda or perhaps double-talk.

However, the Soviets have no monopoly on double-talk. For example, American businessmen talk about excellence but claim no ultimate standard of excellence.

Most definitions of excellence use words like "superior" and "good." The word *excellence* appeals to the highest standard to which our language can aspire.

Psalm 8 speaks of such a standard. First, it points to the origin of excellence. Second, it tells of the absence of God's excellence when man separates himself from God. Third, it shows how the presence of God's excellence can change our lives.

## 1. THE ORIGIN OF EXCELLENCE

Psalm 8 speaks of the origin of excellence. Verse 1 reads:

> O Lord, our Lord,
>   How excellent is Your name in all the earth,
> You who set Your glory above the heavens!

According to the psalmist, the ultimate standard of value is found in God's name. His name is the Bureau of Standards for the entire currency of excellence in heaven and earth. The National Bureau of Standards in Washington, D.C. holds the measurements which all other measurements in the United States must match. Just so, God's name is the standard for our measurements of excellence.

Our problem is that we often measure ourselves against substandard measurements. If you happen to be 5 feet, 11 inches tall and you walk into a classroom of third-graders, you might think of yourself as tall. But step on a college basketball court during afternoon practice and you will see what it really means to be tall.

Excellence operates in the same way. We think our ways approach excellence because we measure ourselves against the dwarflike standards of our world. Too often we compare ourselves to ourselves. However, when we get a vision of God's perfection, our eyes are open wide and we see what excellence is all about.

In Isaiah 40, God called His prophet to enlarge his vision of the excellence of God. Isaiah's vision of God was too small—too human. Therefore, God said to him in verse 25: "To whom then will you liken Me, that I should be his equal?"

As the chapter continues, God instructs Isaiah to compare human achievements with those of God at Creation. Can man measure the water of the seas or the dust of the earth?

Then God tells Isaiah to compare His power with that of any superpower of that day—Assyria, Egypt, and Babylon: "All

21

nations before Him are as nothing (v. 17). God says, "The nations are like a drop in a bucket" (v. 15).

Finally, God asked Isaiah to scan the heavens. In the skies, the prophet saw the most magnificent sight known to man. But God said in Isaiah 40:26:

> Lift up your eyes on high
> And see who has created these things,
> Who brings out their host by number;
> He calls them all by name,
> By the greatness of His might
> And the strength of His power;
> Not one is missing.

God's message to Isaiah was that excellence is most clearly seen in the nature and activity of God. Also, God's message in Psalm 8 is that excellence finds its origin in the name of the Lord. It is His name which reveals His entire character. It declares His greatness. It invites us to worship Him.

The real excellence in our world is not to be found in the corporate headquarters that dot the land. The true source of excellence is the high and holy name of God. Psalm 8 provides the basis and origin of all true excellence.

## 2. THE ABSENCE OF GOD'S EXCELLENCE

What is a man without God's excellent name? The answer is, he is nothing! What was man before God breathed life into the dust of the ground? Man was nonexistent. He had no possibilities at all for excellence.

Verse 4 of Psalm 8 asks:

> What is man that You are mindful of him,
> And the son of man that You visit him?

The answer to this question is "nothing." For, before God

created man, he was dust. And the same holds true of man apart from God after the Creation.

The excellence of man apart from God is not just misguided. It is unfounded and based on counterfeit standards. In a real sense, it is double-talk.

The question, "What is man?" is the question of the twentieth century. But having given up the Bible's answer, philosophers have attempted to provide new answers.

Karl Marx defined man as the sum of his social relations. Freud said that man is the end result of unconscious mental drives. Sartre saw him as the sum of his actions. Each of these men has had a profound influence on our universities. Their ideas betray naturalist assumptions. Man, they believe, is the product of evolutionary forces alone. Their theories have no place for God and they deny His existence.

The direction of our age tends to abandon all references to God's excellence. Its high standard is missing from the boardroom and the classroom. It has been replaced with antitheistic theories which keep God out of their conversations and reduce man to his environment. This is the inevitable result of human definitions of excellence.

We are left with various standards of excellence or no standards at all. Every arena of society then becomes a battleground where my desire to excel runs against yours. There is no cosmic Bureau of Standards which justifies any of our achievements. The absence of God's excellence leaves man floundering in total confusion.

## 3. THE PRESENCE OF GOD'S EXCELLENCE

But consider the presence of God's excellence, for in the presence of His excellence life takes on meaning.

The most striking fact about Psalm 8 is its affirmation that God's excellence makes man and his work important.

After speaking about the God who fashions the heavens with His fingers, this psalm tempts us to say that man counts for nothing in this vast universe of ours. When science began to understand the dimensions of our universe, scientists told people that the earth was not the center of the universe. Many people were thrown into disbelief. Some even let go of their Christian worldview, and with it, a belief in the dignity and importance of man. "How can man be dignified," they said, "if he is a mere cosmic speck?"

But after speaking of heaven's splendor, the psalmist explains how this majestic God has made something glorious of insignificant man. We find that God delights in taking weak men and women to use them to accomplish His sovereign will. In other words, man's significance in the world is not based on his own greatness. Our significance is based on God's calling.

God has chosen to crown weak men and women with a divine excellence. After asking, "What is man?" the psalmist answers his own question:

> For You have made him a little lower than the angels, and You have crowned him with glory and honor (v. 5).

A better translation reads, "Thou hast made man a little lower than God." What a mind-stretching truth! This places upon man a dignified mantle. If there was ever any basis for self-esteem, this is it. God's plan for you and me is to make us His children, who would rule like Himself.

You may be thinking, "But I thought that man was fallen. If so, how can we speak of him as still having such dignity?"

True, man fell from the fellowship and glory he once enjoyed in God's presence. Thus man's capacity for divine excellence has been defaced. However, this does not mean that God's image is wholly lost. It is no longer a functioning image. But the image is still there structurally. The image is defaced—not erased. Man is like a painting from top to bottom. The painting still hangs, but its beauty and original function have been lost.

We need to keep these two facts in mind when we think about man. Man carries God's image: this is where his dignity comes from. This makes us strive for excellence. But man has sinned and flounders in confusion. The good news is that the presence of God's excellence can change our lives. We were meant to excel in the task God gave us. Verses 6 through 8 explains that task:

> You have made him to have dominion
> over the works of Your hands;
> You have put all things under his feet,
> All sheep and oxen—
> Even the beasts of the field,
> The birds of the air,
> And the fish of the sea
> That pass through the paths of the seas.

Think of it, God's purpose for mankind was to rule over all the earth. Man was to be God's keeper of earth's resources and animal life, His land and resource management officer.

Has this assignment ended? No, it has not. While many rebel against this God-given assignment, our calling remains. While many exploit His creation—mismanaging it and appropriating His funds for themselves—the creation task still remains. We fulfill it in our own vocations.

Of which part of God's creation has He made you a manager? It might be an office of three people. It might be your family. It might be a plot of land that you farm or a cattle ranch that you run. It might be only a word processor. It could be five feet on an assembly line. But how do you carry out God's task where you are?

Psalm 8 promises that God has not left us alone to flounder. The fact that His name is excellent and that we bear His name tells us that we too can excel. Furthermore, God has promised to assist us in our task. Verse 4 assures us that the Lord is mindful of us. He deeply cares for us.

Take a look around you now. Consider how well you are doing. Do you have trouble fulfilling God's call? At times we all do.

We understand the call with our minds, but the will does not want to go along. The end result is that often we are poor stewards. We fail to excel. The entire enterprise of ruling earth as God's regent seems sabotaged.

The problem is sin. We are entrenched in our stubborn pride. Instead of managing the world, we leave it mismanaged. What hope is there for our world? Apart from God, we will never experience excellence.

Yet all is not lost. There was another Son of Man who did not fall short of excellence in His life. He learned obedience and fulfilled the calling which we could not. That Man is Jesus Christ the Lord. *obedient unto death*

Our salvation can be in no other name. Here is why. In His life and death, Jesus conquered the very enemies that hinder us from excellence. He defeated sin by being obedient to the point of death. Then He broke death's power by rising from the dead.

In Hebrews 2 the author quotes extensively from Psalm 8, pointing to the One who accomplished His role as the Son of Man. It exalts Jesus who truly fulfilled His role of dominion and showed forth the presence of God's excellence in His life. Hebrews 2:8 states, "You have put all things in subjection under His feet." Verse 9 says this:

> But we see Jesus, who was made a little lower than the angels, for the suffering of death crowned with glory and honor, that He, by the grace of God, might taste death for everyone.

Then verse 10 gives the good news that by His death Jesus brings many sons to glory.

Do you see it? The glory can return. The excellence can

come, but only through trusting Him who has that name above all names—the excellent name of Jesus.

Blind poet Fanny Crosby recognized at an early age that human standards of worth, value, and excellence fall short of God's. At eight or nine years of age she penned these words:

> Oh, what a happy soul I am,
> Although I cannot see,
> I am resolved that in this world
> Contented I will be.
>
> How many blessings I enjoy
> That other people don't!
> To weep and sigh because I'm blind
> I cannot nor I won't.

Even at this tender age, she recognized that the ultimate source of excellence is in Jesus Christ.

Is your standard of excellence in Jesus Christ? Is it in His death that you find self-worth? Or are you still beating your own path to a substandard measure?

Psalm 8, after describing what we were meant to be, returns to the source of all excellence. The last verse repeats the first as a recognition that all human excellence begins and ends with the Lord: "O Lord, our Lord, how excellent is Your name in all the earth!"

## REMEMBER

God's message in Psalm 8 is that excellence finds its origin in the name of the Lord.

The excellence of man apart from God is not just misguided. It is unfounded, based on counterfeit standards.

The most striking thing about Psalm 8 is its affirmation that God's excellence makes man and his work important.

God delights in taking weak things like men and using them

to accomplish His will.

The fact that His name is excellent and that we bear His name says that we too can excel.

*God works things for His good.*

*Verses Psalm 46:1-2, Ro 8: 31, 37, 1 Cor 10:13*
*1 Cor 10:13  Heb 2:9-18*
*1 Peter 2:24-25  Heb 4:14-16*
*James 1:3, 6-9, 4:12-19*

*Does He work in the life of Non-Christians?*

# CHAPTER THREE

# GOD IS STILL
# ON THE THRONE

*1 Peter & Psalm 9:4 = how much does God ~~permits~~ protect us / judge / make things right vs us defending ourselves?  Psalm 139*

## Psalm 9

Psalm 9 is a hymn for the twentieth century. Its words fit the dilemmas of the nuclear age as much as they do those of the ancient world. Psalm 9 concludes with these words from verses 17-20:

> The wicked shall be turned into hell,
> And all the nations forget God.
> For the needy shall not always be forgotten;
> The expectation of the poor shall not perish forever.
> Arise, O Lord,
> Do not let men prevail;
> Let the nations be judged in Your sight.
> Put them in fear, O Lord,
> That the nations may know themselves
>     to be but men.

We do not overstate the facts when we say that our twentieth century has been a violent century. We have seen the rise of

*NOTE: God is the final judge. He is in control. SURRENDER my will*

29

totalitarianism, two world wars, and at least 128 limited wars since 1945. Such statistics are bone-chilling.

About 11 million people died as a result of Hitler's exterminations. Six million of those were Jews. Unfortunately, these figures pale in comparison to our times. In the United States, since the Supreme Court's 1973 Roe vs. Wade decision, 18 million babies have been aborted. The international figure since 1945 pushes that number to well over 50 million. We have aborted about as many lives as were killed in all of World War II.

But the story gets worse! The Marxist revolutions in Cambodia, China, and the Soviet Union, and the expansion of Communist rule, mark the most tragic acts of our times. At least 27 million people were wiped out in the Communist revolutions of China. A conservative figure for Stalin's purges in the USSR stands at 29 million. Alexander Solzhenitsyn says that between 1917 and the present, over 100 million of his countrymen were exterminated.

These numbers are difficult to comprehend. But they rule out any idea that mankind is improving! These facts tell us that we have regressed. If any age should be called a "dark age," it is ours. And all of this has occurred without unleashing our nuclear arsenal. The twentieth century abounds in tragic detail of man's inhumanity to man.

Have you ever wrestled with the problem of suffering? History is strewn with victims who "got in the way" of ambitious men and parties. The Old Testament character Job wrestled with the suffering of the innocent. So did the Psalmist David.

Psalm 9 provides an explanation of how David could sing to God in the darkness of night. He could sing because he believed that history was incomplete. For David, God was in control. Christians affirm the same today. Reciting the Apostle's Creed, we agree that Christ will "come to judge the living and the dead."

Three main characters come to the forefront in Psalm 9: the

victim, the oppressor, and the judge. Look at each of these as we consider the subject of the judgment.

## 1. THE VICTIM

Consider the victim: who was he? In Psalm 9 the victim is the psalmist and those who stand with him. At times, David speaks in personal terms. He says in verse 4 that God has maintained "my right and my cause." He speaks of "my enemies" (v. 3), and "my trouble" (v. 13). In other places, David generalizes and speaks of "the oppressed" (v. 9) and "the humble" (v. 12).

Verse 10 tells us something about the character of those victims. Who are they? They are God-seekers:

> And those who know Your name will
> put their trust in You;
> For You, Lord, have not forsaken
> those who seek You.

Simply, these victims find their refuge in the Lord.

What was their situation? David gives no historical details. However, verse 4 describes them as innocent. It speaks of a right and a cause. These people are falsely persecuted. Verse 12 implies that their blood has been shed. Some are hated and hunted to death's door. They are trampled and soon forgotten. Wicked men and women prevail.

In this life the righteous in Jesus Christ—"the good guys"— do not always win. Sometimes we go through the fire. Remember, Jesus was crucified. Peter and Paul were murdered. Early Christians faced wild animals. Some modern Christians have known the slow death of Nazi prison camps and Russian jails. Some, like Covenant missionary Paul Carlson, have been gunned down. Others in the public sphere try to maintain Christian integrity, only to be run over. They are victimized.

The natural response of the victim is to cry out for help. The victims of Psalm 9 call, "Have mercy on me, O Lord! Consider my trouble from those who hate me" (v. 13).

Sometimes God delivers in just the way we ask. The Exodus stands out as a good example. But sometimes God allows us to suffer for reasons that are known only to Him. In fact, Jesus told His disciples to expect the same suffering He experienced. They were to daily take up their cross and follow Him.

In 1940, after the fall of the Netherlands and Belgium, Nazi troops broke through to the coast of the English Channel at Dunkirk. They circled 330,000 British and French soldiers. Had these allies surrendered, the war would have taken a tragic turn. Through an amazing display of courage, a secret flotilla of boats rescued the soldiers. Before that rescue, in a bleak hour, the stranded British troops sent a message back to their homeland. It simply read, "But if not . . . "

Evidently the Nazis never understood that message, but an Englishman familiar with the *King James* Bible would. The words "but if not" are the first three words of Daniel, chapter 3, verse 18. In this passage, Daniel's three friends Shadrach, Meshach, and Abednego were about to be thrown into the fiery furnace because they would not serve the god of King Nebuchadnezzar. These victims spoke out to the king and said:

> O Nebuchadnezzar, . . . our God whom we serve is able to deliver us from the burning fiery furnace, and He will deliver us from your hand, O king. *But if not,* let it be known to you, O king, that we do not serve your gods, nor will we worship the gold image which you have set up (Daniel 3:16-18).

Daniel's friends were innocent victims. They knew that God was able to deliver them from their fiery ordeal. Yet they prayed as Christians pray, "Thy will be done." They understood that sometimes God has other plans to promote His glory.

In Psalm 9, we find David praising God *in the fire*. Like Shadrach, Meshach, and Abednego, David knew that God's justice will prevail, and that sooner or later the righteous will be vindicated.

The victims in Psalm 9 are encouraged to "take heart." When the situation looks utterly impossible, they are told to look up and believe, because God will deliver. They are called to lift up God's name and declare His deeds among the people (verse 11).

In verses 3 through 6, David refers to God's past deliverance. In verses 7 through 16, he speaks of God's future deliverance. Here we find help for ourselves today. When hope is lost, we too are to consider the name of our redeeming God. We are to look back on His saving work in history and look forward to His future deliverance. Remembering the past is a great source of strength and encouragement.

Do you have any memorials in your life to help you remember God's loving-kindness? Israel did. At the Passover Feast, they thought carefully and deeply about God's deliverance from Egyptian bondage. Their past deliverance by God encouraged them to march each day into the future.

Looking to the future is also a source of joy and strength to believers. Christians know that Christ will come again and rule in righteousness.

In Psalm 9 the Children of Israel reviewed their trials in light of past and future deliverance. This gave them strength and courage. They learned to *replay* God's care as they had seen it in history, and to preplay His promises as they looked to the future. This holy example should characterize our response to the tough trials of life.

Have you been victimized? Or do you know someone who is victimized? It is helpful to remember that the story is not over until God speaks the last word in judgment. Therefore, wait patiently on the Lord.

## 2. THE OPPRESSOR

The second subject of Psalm 9 is the oppressor. Ultimately our oppressor is Satan. But Satan has many workers. He has an army of villains whom he employed in history—Hitler, Stalin, Gadhafi, and many others who receive far less publicity. And he has a host of demons at his disposal as well.

The oppressor often appears as a political savior—an angel of light. He promotes his own glory, not God's. In forgetting the one, true God, he makes himself god. Totalitarian systems, even though they claim to be nonreligious, are really secular religious forms replacing Christianity. Nazism is a religion of race; Marxism, a religion of class. It is no coincidence that in Marxist countries images of Lenin, Marx, and some national revolutionary hero are found in every town. They are promoted as objects of worship. To them is ascribed the kingdom, the power, and the glory. They steal the glory that belongs to God alone.

Who were Satan's partners in Psalm 9? David simply describes them as "the nations" and "the wicked"—those who stood against God's anointed king and abused His people. What did these oppressors do? First of all, they forgot God (v. 17). They also set traps for the righteous (v. 15). They caused suffering (v. 18) and at times exterminated the innocent (v. 12). For a while they seemed to get away with it. At times their victory seemed complete. Before the defeat of the Third Reich, membership in the German National Socialist Party brought prestige, power, and in some cases, wealth. For a time they enjoyed all the privileges of Europe.

But the discovery of this membership roll by the allies after the war brought terror to those whose names were on it. It testified against them at the Nuremberg Trials. It brought criminal investigation and prison for many, as well as death for others. Their season had come to an abrupt end, and that is the fate of all oppressors.

Verse 18 implies that the oppressors forget the needy. This could mean that they ignore them. But more than likely, it means that they lose their memory. Their victims are wiped out. And when the oppressor records history, the victims are not only physically gone, but their memory is wiped out as well.

This reminds us of modern practices. In George Orwell's novel *1984*, the all-powerful state alters the history books to hide its crimes. It destroys old records. In effect, it removes all memory of opposition to the state.

The way modern Soviet history is written confirms Orwell's prophecies. They erase the memory of opposition so that people will lose a standard of comparison. Indeed, one of the things that kept Solzhenitsyn alive in the Russian prison camps was his desire to record and keep alive the memory of the millions who were executed. He did this in his memoirs.

Psalm 9 reminds us that the havoc of the oppressor is only temporary. Verse 3 says, "They shall fall and perish at Your presence." In other words, when confronted with true power and glory, the counterfeits go to pieces.

### 3. THE JUDGE

The most prominent presence in Psalm 9 is Almighty God, the Judge. The psalmist says in verse 4: "You sat on the throne judging in righteousness." Then in verses 8 and 9, he goes on to say:

> He shall judge the world in righteousness,
> And He shall administer judgment for
>    the peoples in uprightness.
> The Lord also will be a refuge for the oppressed,
> A refuge in times of trouble.

The psalm reminds us that the actions of men do not go unnoticed. God sees! Whatever a person sows, that will they reap. The sin and horror of our age has been recorded in detail. God has kept His own memoir. The idea that we can get away with what others do not see is an outright lie. God's judgment is inescapable.

Of the Judge, verse 5 says:

You have rebuked the nations,
You have destroyed the wicked;
You have blotted out their name forever and ever.

God's judgment is swift and total. He visits them with a wrath more intense than their own. Verse 6 says:

O enemy, destructions are finished forever!
And you have destroyed cities;
Even their memory has perished.

In this last statement, we see an amazing reversal. It says the needy will not be forgotten. Rather, the oppressor will enter oblivion. The nations which forgot God will themselves be forgotten. They will be consigned to the ash heap of history. Verse 17 says they will return to hell (Sheol), the place of the dead. This is their destiny. Death is their native element. For in the end, our deeds reflect our relationship to God. The very breath of the wicked smells like death. They have chosen to be without God.

The victims of Psalm 9, on the other hand, love and trust the Lord. They need not fear judgment. Their deeds testify to their right relationship to God. They are safe within God's stronghold. It will be for them as for David, "The Lord . . . will be a refuge . . . in times of trouble" (v. 9). The refuge refers to a stronghold, a place of high fortification. This is what the Lord is to you and me.

In 1527, Martin Luther entered into an agonizing spiritual depression. It was during this "dark night of the soul" that he wrote his most famous hymn, "A Mighty Fortress Is Our God":

A mighty fortress is our God,
A bulwark never failing;

36

Our helper He amid the flood
Of mortal ills prevailing.

For still our ancient foe
Doth seek to work us woe;
His craft and power are great,
And, armed with cruel hate,
On earth is not his equal.

Did we in our own strength confide,
Our striving would be losing;
Were not the right man on our side,
The man of God's own choosing:
Dost ask who that may be?
Christ Jesus, it is He;
Lord Sab-a-oth His name,
From age to age the same,
And He must win the battle.

Luther's third stanza speaks of a world filled with evil and threatening to undo us. But then in stanza four, he reminds us that men may kill our mortal body, but God's truth abides still.

For Luther, the great evils of history have been answered. Jesus Christ has won the ultimate battle. The oppressors have been defeated and will be judged. David experienced this same confidence of victory.

We Christians also have the crucifixion and resurrection of Christ to help see us through the tragedies of history. This is God's answer to the problem of evil and suffering. On the cross, God the Judge lowered Himself to become *the victim*. There Jesus suffered at the hands of His oppressors. It seems as if all was lost. But on the third day, Jesus triumphantly arose from the grave. He defeated the powers of sin and death. And just as God brought good out of evil at Calvary, so He can do it in the lives of each of us who trust in Him.

All the holocausts of history have been addressed by the cross of Jesus Christ. Their root has been dug out and destroyed by Christ's great victory. But the holocausts will be addressed again on the Day of Judgment when all must answer for their deeds before God.

Horatio G. Spafford lost all his earthly possessions in the great Chicago Fire of 1871. While he attempted to rebuild his business life, he sent his wife and daughters back to England. As they were crossing the Atlantic Ocean, their ship was struck broadside by another ship. Mrs. Spafford watched helplessly as her daughters were swept overboard and lost in the ocean. Upon hearing the shocking news, Horatio set out for England to be with his wife. He went out on deck as the ship approached the area where his daughters had drowned. As it moved across their watery grave, he began to pen the words of a beloved Gospel song.

When peace like a river attendeth my way,
   When sorrows like sea billows roll;
Whatever my lot, Thou hast taught me to say,
   "It is well, it is well with my soul."

Though Satan should buffet, tho' trials should come,
   Let this blest assurance control,
That Christ has regarded my helpless estate,
   And hath shed His own blood for my soul.

My sin—oh, the bliss of this glorious thought,
   My sin—not in part, but the whole,
Is nailed to the cross and I bear it no more,
   Praise the Lord, praise the Lord, O my soul!

And, Lord, haste the day when the faith shall be
   sight,
   The clouds be rolled back as a scroll,

The trump shall resound and the Lord shall descend,
  "Even so," it is well with my soul.


## REMEMBER

David could sing because he believed that history was incomplete. For David, God was in control.

Sometimes God delivers in just the way we ask. But sometimes He allows us to suffer for reasons known only to Him.

Christians have the crucifixion and the resurrection of Christ to help them see through the tragedies of history.

The holocausts will be addressed again on the Day of Judgment when all must answer for their deeds before God.

# CHAPTER FOUR

# How God Communicates

## PSALM 19

P salm 19 is a beautiful poem about communications, and yet it has nothing to do with television networks or AT&T. The theme of Psalm 19 is the most important kind of communication conceivable. It speaks about communication between Almighty God and men and women. We call this communication "revelation."

Creation bears witness to God's revelation. His creatures in turn receive and reflect what God is like, much as an antenna reflects the beam of a radio transmitter or the moon reflects the light of the sun.

But what does this communication between God and His creation have to do with you and me? Psalm 19 answers that question by presenting three witnesses: the witness of nature, the witness of God's Law, and the witness of His servant.

### 1. THE WITNESS OF NATURE

The psalmist presents the witness of God through nature in verses 1-6 of Psalm 19. We see God's general revelation through creation in the heavens, the skies, the day, the night, the earth, and the sun. All send out a message. They speak about God's glory. They announce God's reputation. Psalm 19 begins with these beautiful words:

> The heavens declare the glory of God;
> And the firmament shows His handiwork.
> Day unto day utters speech,
> And night unto night reveals knowledge.

The heavens in all their expanse announce God's ability as Creator. David tells us that the galaxies speak to us—oh, not verbally as we speak to one another, but they do proclaim the Creator and send out an articulate message. They mirror God Himself.

The orderliness and perfection of the solar system becomes a school where men learn something about God's character. They demonstrate that God is a God of intricate design; a God who organized the universe to operate in accordance with a master plan. Creation tells of a God of beauty; One who delights in harmony, color, and form.

The word for "man" in the Greek language is the word *anthropos*, which means "the uplooking one." Have you ever gazed into a clear night's sky and looked at the stars? God intended for us to "look up and consider His creation." We are the "uplooking one." A dog looks down, a cow looks down, a horse looks down, but men and women were created by God to look up to God and view His glorious creation. The heavens eloquently announce that God is alive, well, and active.

James, in the New Testament, reminds us that "every good gift and every perfect gift is from above, and comes down from the Father of lights" (James 1:17).

Of course, while the heavens constantly tell of the glory of God, not everyone receives this message. As with radio and television, a transmitter without a receiver is useless! The networks can send out the finest in programming, but it is useless to you unless you tune in and receive it. God sends out information, but you must receive that information and act upon it. He continually sends out mercy and peace, love and forgiveness; but you will never know about it until you are tuned in. David tuned into God's revelation and heard the eloquence of nature's witness.

Psalm 19 goes on to say that both day and night pour forth speech. The regular rotation of the earth elicits a song from the day and an answer from the night. The call of day and the response of night answer one another like a full orchestra where the string section responds to the woodwinds. They speak clearly of the existence of God.

Psalm 19:3 reads, "There is no speech nor language where their voice is not heard." In other words, the evidence of God is everywhere. Verse 4 continues: "Their line has gone out through all the earth, and their words to the end of the world."

No wonder mankind is basically religious. Even the most primitive of cultures have some form of religion. Men and women know they have been spoken to. God's voice is heard "to the end of the world." That is why the Apostle Paul in the Epistle to the Romans says:

> For since the creation of the world His invisible attributes are clearly seen, being understood by the things that are made, even His eternal power and Godhead, so that they are without excuse (1:20).

There is no place in this universe one can go without confronting this witness. Therefore, everyone can hear the testimony of nature. The Holy Spirit concludes, "They are without excuse." Hymnist Stuart K. Hine captured something of the awe and wonder of the witness of nature in his hymn "How Great Thou Art":

# How God Communicates

O Lord my God, when I in awesome wonder
   Consider all the worlds Thy hands have made,
I see the stars, I hear the rolling thunder,
   Thy power throughout the universe displayed.

When through the woods and forest glades I wander
   And hear the birds sing sweetly in the trees;
When I look down from lofty mountain grandeur
   And hear the brook and feel the gentle breeze,

Then sings my soul, my Saviour God, to Thee,
   How great Thou art! How great Thou art!*

Verses 1-6 of Psalm 19 speak about the witness of nature. Creation testifies about God's existence and sovereignty.

## 2. THE WITNESS OF GOD'S LAW

The psalmist moves from creation to God's Law. God's Law consists of His moral commands. They are founded on His moral character. Spoken, they become His Word.

David's praise for the Law of God even exceeds his praise for nature. But you ask, why do we need a special written revelation?

The Book of Genesis tells how Adam and Eve lost their moral innocence in the Garden of Eden. They disobeyed God, clouding their vision of right and wrong. Their eyes became darkened and their hearing dulled. They were now, in a sense, insensitive to the witness of nature. They needed the witness of God's written law to restore their awareness.

Beginning at verse 7 of Psalm 19, the name for God has changed. No longer is the general Hebrew word used as in verses 1 through 6; but now David uses the word *Yahweh*. This name speaks of the God who forgives and the God who redeems

His people.

The witness of creation is great, but we need to explicitly hear the witness of God's Law. Consider Psalm 19:7-9:

> The Law of the Lord is perfect,
>     converting the soul;
> The testimony of the Lord is sure,
>     making wise the simple;
> The statutes of the Lord are right,
>     rejoicing the heart;
> The commandment of the Lord is
>     pure, enlightening the eyes;
> The fear of the Lord is clean,
>     enduring forever;
> The judgments of the Lord are true
>     and righteous altogether.

David here writes that God's Law is perfect (verse 7). Like the temple sacrifices, God's Law is without blemish. Contrary to man-made laws, God's Law never needs to be amended.

God's Law is sure (verse 7). In an unsure world, God's Law is reliable. It provides a fixed point of reference amid a fast-changing world. The Law of the Lord makes one wise.

Verse 8 reads, "The statutes of the Lord are right." God's Law is a foundation for all that is right. Here one finds true righteousness.

Verse 9 continues, "The fear of the Lord is clean. . . . The judgments of the Lord are true and righteous altogether." In God's Law we find the basis of truth and an unspotted rule.

A good question for us to ask ourselves is this: "How does the Law of God affect me?"

Verse 7 says that it converts the soul. God's Word changes the inner person. It converts. It makes us Godlike. Even today, through the reading of God's Word, we are converted.

Verse 8 tells us that God's Law rejoices the heart and en-

44

lightens the eyes. The eyes represent the mind. Keeping God's Law cleans the mind by purging it of natural darkness.

And finally, in verse 9, the Law is said to have enduring qualities—God's truth abides forever.

In our home, newspapers get stacked on the porch. By evening the morning news makes a soft bed for our Labrador puppy, Schatzie. The daily news does not endure, nor does it heal or revive. In fact, the daily news is downright depressing.

David sums up the witness of God's words in verse 10: "More to be desired are they than gold . . . sweeter also than honey." The people of that day found great satisfaction in the taste of honey and the possession of gold. David says, "God's Law has greater value and appeal than gold or honey."

### 3. THE WITNESS OF GOD'S SERVANT

As David considers God's creation and God's Law, he is overwhelmed by his own sinfulness. In verse 12 he asks, "Who can understand his errors?" Here David speaks of himself. He senses his sinfulness and his need for cleansing. Then he prays, "Cleanse me from secret faults." He prays in verse 13: "Keep back your servant also from presumptuous sins; let them not have dominion over me."

We too, in the presence of God's mighty works and God's holy Word, plead with Isaiah:

> Woe is me, for I am undone! Because I am a man of unclean lips, and I dwell in the midst of a people of unclean lips; for my eyes have seen the King, the Lord of hosts (6:5).

The goal of David's confession was that he would be blameless—just like the other witnesses of Psalm 19. In the closing verse, his prayer was this:

> Let the words of my mouth

and the meditation of my heart
Be acceptable in Your sight,
O Lord, my strength and my redeemer.

David wanted to participate in this hymn of praise. Like the heavens, he wanted to proclaim the glory of God. Like the Law, he wanted to be righteous altogether. David longed to communicate the Lord in everything he was and did.

In our technological anxiousness to speak, we have often lost the all-important message. It has been lost amid the information. We have an abundance of words. They multiply on our computer screens and in our publications, but so does our ignorance of the Word—God's revelation.

## REMEMBER

Creation bears witness to God's revelation like the moon reflects the light of the sun.

Men and women were created by God to look up to God and view His glorious creation.

The orderliness and perfection of the solar system becomes a school where men learn something about God's character.

The call of day and the response of night answer one another like a full orchestra where the string section responds to the woodwinds.

God's Law consists of His moral commands. They are founded on His moral character. Spoken, they become His Word.

The goal of David's confession was that he would be blameless—just like the other witnesses of Psalm 19.

All of us who name the name of Christ should make verse 14 the prayer of our hearts.

Let the words of my mouth
and the meditation of my heart
Be acceptable in Your sight,
O Lord, my strength and my redeemer.

# CHAPTER FIVE

# THE LORD IS MY SHEPHERD

## PSALM 23

Empires and countries often adopt various animals to symbolize their national spirit. The Roman Empire chose the wingspread eagle. The United States claims the same symbol. The British Empire selected the kingly lion. Russia picked the powerful bear. In each case the animal signifies strength and independence.

In the Bible we find, to the surprise of some, that God represents His people by a lamb, an animal that needs a shepherd.

Spurgeon called Psalm 23, "the pearl of psalms." Alexander Maclaren said, "The world could get along without many a large book better than this sunny little psalm." It is one of the first passages of the Bible that children hear and memorize. Refresh your mind and heart by reading it once again:

The Lord is my shepherd;
I shall not want.
He makes me to lie down in green pastures;

He leads me beside the still waters.
He restores my soul;
He leads me in the paths of righteousness
For His name's sake.
Yea, though I walk through the valley
    of the shadow of death,
I will fear no evil;
For You are with me;
Your rod and Your staff, they comfort me.
You prepare a table before me in the
    presence of my enemies;
You anoint my head with oil;
My cup runs over.
Surely goodness and mercy shall follow me
All the days of my life;
And I will dwell in the house of the Lord
Forever.

This psalm provides us with two inspiring pictures. Verses 1-4 portray God as a Shepherd, and we as His sheep. Verses 5-6 present God as a gracious Host, and we as His guests. In this study, I want to focus on the first picture of the Shepherd and His sheep.

Over 400 times the Bible refers to sheep. This tells us that if we want to learn about the people of God, we need to carefully observe the habits of sheep. However, that is easier said than done in our urban society. To really understand this psalm, we must journey out of urban America to a society that depends on sheep.

You can still see thousands of sheep in England. Palestine, however, did not have the lush English meadows nor its wet climate. Instead, a rocky, dry land mass and a blazing sun provided the setting. During the summertime, the heat scorched the grass and dried up many of the water holes. In such times, wells had to be used.

48

A conscientious sheep farmer will tell you that sheep require endless attention. Shepherding them demands more than merely leaving them on their own. Sheep are not very bright. They are almost defenseless and continually in need of protection. They need constant provision of food and rest. They easily stray. A conscientious shepherd devotes himself to these weak and dependent creatures. And all this pictures exactly what the Lord does for you and me. He provides, He directs, and He protects. This psalm looks at these three areas of God's care.

## 1. THE SHEPHERD PROVIDES

Consider how the Shepherd provides for His sheep:

> The Lord is my shepherd;
> I shall not want.
> He makes me to lie down in green pastures;
> He leads me beside the still waters.

The words "*I shall not want*" constitute a confession—a sheep's confession. It means, "I lack nothing"; it speaks of a sheep perfectly content with its shepherd.

What do sheep need? Verses 2-3 tell us they need green pastures and quiet waters. Sheep need food, water, and peace. The shepherd provides all three. He seeks out choice grazing land for his flock. If he just left them in the same field, they would eat all the grass away. So the shepherd keeps new pastures in mind for his sheep.

Then, the shepherd brings them to quiet waters. When the grass burns under the scorching sun, the shepherd leads them to water. Some translate "quiet waters" to mean "quieted waters." In other words, he takes waters from the rushing stream and dams up a small pool away from the rush and turbulence. There the sheep will not be frightened by the fast-moving current. They can drink without fear.

In the Old Testament, the Children of Israel wandered very

much like sheep in the wilderness, and God took care of their basic needs too. He provided food, water, and rest. When Israel complained about hunger, God sent manna from heaven. When Israel complained about thirst, He provided water from a rock. When Israel was weary and oppressed in Egypt, God delivered His people and brought them to the Promised Land. God provided a way out of their struggles. He also provided all along the way and ultimately all the way till they were in the land.

For every need you will ever have, God is adequate. As our Shepherd He provides.

God's provision in Psalm 23 has to do specifically with the soul. Verse 3 says, "He restores my soul." And the questions we have to ask ourselves are: What provision is there for my soul? Have we received the Living Bread of Life? Are we drinking that which cannot quench our soul's thirst? Are we dissatisfied with the momentary resting places of this life and longing for something that will last? Remember the Shepherd provides for his own. Can you confidently say, "The Lord is *my* Shepherd"? The Lord wants to have a personal relationship with each one.

## 2. THE SHEPHERD DIRECTS

Not only does God the Shepherd provide, He also directs. Verse 2 says, "He leads me beside still waters." Verse 3 says, "He leads me in the paths of righteousness for His name's sake."

Have you ever seen sheep on a hill? They wander haphazardly, caring only for the next clump of grass. They easily stray. Palestine had not only the natural danger of wandering, but the danger of getting on the wrong path. Some paths were worn by travelers, some by bandits, some by the winds. If a defenseless sheep strayed too far or took the wrong path, it would be exposed to all sorts of dangers—dangers of the night, predators, and darkened cliffs.

The Good Shepherd watches over and keeps track of His own. He counts the sheep. The New Testament says that if He sees even one lamb missing, He leaves the others in safety to search after the one which is lost (Matt. 18:12).

One of the unique features of an Eastern shepherd is that, unlike the Western cattleman, he does not drive his flock. Rather, he leads them. He establishes such an intimacy with them that they recognize his voice and his appearance. They trust him and follow after him.

If there happens to be a sheep that does not cooperate, the shepherd watches it closely, disciplining it with his staff. If things fail to improve, sometimes the shepherd will actually break the sheep's leg and then nurse him back to health. The sheep will then become more dependent upon the shepherd. The shepherd knows that an independent sheep is a sheep in great danger.

In the Old Testament, God was a Shepherd to Israel. He did not drive His people out of Egypt—He led them. He went before them with a pillar of cloud by day and a pillar of fire by night. He also gave them His Word in the form of the Law. Like the shepherd's voice, they were to recognize it and listen to its call. But more, God appointed tenant shepherds over His flock once they reached the Promised Land. But as Ezekiel 34 tells us, these shepherds often cared for themselves rather than for the flock. God then stood against the shepherds and vowed to deliver and care for the sheep Himself.

In the New Testament, God directed His people by sending them His Son, Jesus, the Good Shepherd. Jesus Christ promises to lead His flock to abundant life. He guides us by His written Word and the Holy Spirit. Jesus also appointed tenant shepherds when He ascended into heaven. He told His apostles, "Feed My sheep." Those who pass on the apostles' teaching are called "pastors," which literally means "herdsmen" or "shepherds."

But what about us now? We are all on some path. Whose lead will you follow? Is the Lord your Shepherd? If He is your shepherd then follow Him.

In his book *How Shall We Then Live*, Francis Schaeffer told of the confession of modern-day sheep. The modern secular mind has abandoned God as Shepherd. First such a person says, "I am my own shepherd." This is the voice of secular humanism which sees man as the measure of all things. Second, he says, "Sheep are my shepherd." This voice speaks of those who have sworn to follow the heroes of our age, or the voice of the majority. Third, there comes the cry that "everything is my shepherd." This is the confession of those who worshiped life itself in various forms of pantheism. And finally, disillusioned with all of these, some have despaired in a confession that "Nothing is my shepherd." This is the voice of the nihilists—those who say that existence is senseless, and there is no ground for truth or morals.

What is your confession? Whom do you follow? P.T. Forsyth, the English theologian, said that the purpose of life is not to find our freedom, but to find our Master. Only when we find our Master is our freedom clearly defined. Only when we choose the shepherd do we discover where we may safely graze. Who is your shepherd? The answer is to choose Christ and follow His directions.

## 3. THE SHEPHERD PROTECTS

A good shepherd not only provides and directs, but he also protects his sheep. We read that David as a shepherd boy fought and killed a lion and a bear which threatened his flock. Look at verse 4 of Psalm 23:

> Yea, though I walk through the valley
>     of the shadow of death,
> I will fear no evil;
> For You are with me;
> Your rod and Your staff,
>     they comfort me.

Sometimes to get to the best pastures in the high country the shepherd has to lead his flock through the valley. The valley in

Psalm 23 is literally one of deep shadows. In the dark ravines beasts and robbers hide, poised to attack. The more threatening the darkness, the more the sheep need to stay close to the shepherd. But the good shepherd remains with the sheep in the darkness. He is equipped with a rod and staff to protect the sheep.

The rod was a club. It was used to drive away animals and sometimes to examine the skin and wool of the sheep. It could be swung or thrown. For instance, suppose a sheep wandered too close to a bush of poison weeds. The shepherd would throw the rod at the bush to scare the sheep away.

The staff was a pole with a hook on it. It was not so much a defensive weapon as a tool of discipline. The hook could pull the sheep back if it were straying toward danger. The shepherd used it to direct and discipline his sheep with occasional tugs and nudges.

In Old Testament times, the danger to Israel was not wolves and lions, but its national enemies. God the Shepherd promised Israel that He would protect His flock from these enemies if they would listen to His word. He comforted Israel with His presence in the many dark valleys it faced—like the valley of captivity in exile. It was a gracious God who gave release and protection. God promised them a land and a nation under a coming Messiah who would make Israel a great light to the world.

In the New Testament, God provides His shepherdly protection through the Lord Jesus Christ. The Gospels, however, see the enemy not as a nation, but the evil one and his domain. The enemy is sin and holds mankind in chains. It was against this enemy that Jesus promised His protection to us, for He defeated Satan and the power of sin and death by His victory on the cross.

In Luke 12, Jesus warned men not to seek after life in the body as an end in itself. "Do not worry about your life" (v. 22), He said, "but seek the kingdom of God, and all these things shall be added to you" (v. 31). Then He took up the sheep metaphor and said, "Do not fear, little flock, for it is your Father's good pleasure to give you the kingdom."

My friend, whose protection do you seek? Are all your bets on this life?

Life is full of both high pastures and deep valleys. Of all the valleys, the darkest is the valley of death. But Psalm 23 offers a bright hope to all believers. Death is a passable valley. You can go through it.

What are your fears? The psalmist said, "I will fear no evil." He meant that he would not be paralyzed by any circumstance of life. What are you afraid of? Is it death or fear of terminal illness? Is it nuclear war? Is it a fear of growing up or growing old? Is it a fear of nighttime, or heights, or crowded places? David said, "I will fear no evil; for You are with me" (Ps. 23:4).

The presence of the Lord gave David great courage. He had plenty of valleys in his lifetime. He faced the darkness of the night as a shepherd boy. He encountered wild beasts. He fought giant obstacles of life—like Goliath. He suffered through the rebellion of his son Absalom, that valley of a rebellious child. He agonized at the death of his baby. He felt the hot, ruthless pursuit of his life by his superior, Saul. And his heart was broken when his son Amnon committed incest with his sister. Yes, David had plenty of deep dark valleys.

A right-minded sheep recognizes that it is defenseless against its enemies. That is why it stays close to the shepherd.

This is what David did. The Christian must do the same. The church is called a "flock" in the New Testament, not a den of lions! Not a nest of eagles! Our name calls attention to our utter dependency. If people everywhere were honest, they would have to admit that they are sheeplike too. You see, the church is realistic enough to admit that some valleys are too much for it. In our own strength, we cannot make it, especially in death.

The great thing about Jesus our Shepherd is that He went through the valley of death in a way like no one has ever done.

He went in by the most cruel sort of death, but He came out by the most glorious victory. Death could not keep the sinless Son of God. Though it tried, it proved no match for Him. And there on the cross, Jesus defeated this most vicious beast that ever lurked in any dark valleys. He conquered death and rose again.

But more, Jesus promises to each of His own eternal life. It is this eternal safety to which the Bible ultimately refers. We lean on everlasting arms. We follow in Christ's death by dying to our sin.

Have you considered God the Shepherd and His Son, Jesus? There is no one who provides, directs, or protects like Him.

In modern-day shepherding, shepherds sometimes identify sheep by putting a mark in their ear. They cut into one of the ears of the sheep so that it can be quickly identified. This is called an "earmark." It causes some pain for the sheep, but the pain insures that many benefits will follow in the good shepherd's care.

So in dying to our own selfish will, in renouncing that we are our own shepherds, there is some pain; there is cost. But dying to ourselves is nothing compared to the blessings of having God's earmark. This very day, Jesus longs to lead us to green pastures beside quiet waters.

### REMEMBER

A conscientious shepherd devotes himself to these weak and dependent creatures.

For every need you will ever have, there is God's provision.

The New Testament says that if He sees even one lamb missing, He leaves the others in safety to search after the one that is lost.

"The purpose of life is not to find our freedom but to find our Master." —P.T. Forsyth

Psalm 23 offers hope to all. Death is a passable valley.

The greatest thing about Jesus our Shepherd is that He went through the valley of death in a way like no one has ever done.

# CHAPTER SIX

# THE CONFESSION OF SIN

## PSALM 32

A man's very highest moment," said English writer Oscar Wilde, "is when he kneels in the dust and beats his breast and tells the sins of his life." Christians call this admission of sin "confession."

Confession and sin are inseparably linked. The word *confession* means to acknowledge. *Random House Dictionary* defines "confession" as "the disclosure of sinfulness."

A lot of people in our day feel openly uncomfortable with the word *sin*, and yet, try as we may, everyone must believe in sin. Day after day the daily newspapers and news on the airwaves remind us that things are wrong in our world—so wrong that we lock our homes and cars, so wrong that we avoid certain neighborhoods and stay off the streets at certain hours.

Chesterton said, "There is a bias in man like the bias in [a] bowl; and Christianity is the discovery of how to correct the bias." Augustine tells us how deep this bias runs. He wrote, "Before Thee, O God, none is free from sin, not even the infant who has lived a day upon the earth." The old New England primer for grade school children taught "in Adam's fall, we sinned all. . . ."

Psalm 32 uses three words to describe this bias in man's nature: "Transgression," "sin," and "iniquity." To "transgress" is to cut across the boundaries. The word *sin* means "to miss the mark." "Iniquity" speaks of an absence of respect for God's Law.

Psalm 32 assumes the sinfulness of all men and women:

> Blessed is he whose transgression is forgiven,
> Whose sin is covered.
> Blessed is the man to whom
>   the Lord does not impute iniquity,
> And in whose spirit there is no guile (vv. 1-2).

The psalmist is writing about sin, transgressions, and iniquity. He tells us that sin and guilt can be forgiven. This is the good news of Psalm 32.

### 1. SOME IGNORE SIN

David chose to ignore his sin. He sinned and then tried to brush it aside. Read his words and see if you have ever felt as he did.

> When I kept silent, my bones grew old
> Through my groaning all the day long.
> For day and night Your hand was heavy upon me;
> My vitality was turned into the drought
>   of summer (vv. 3-4).

Have you ever felt weighted down because of wrong you had done? David did. Have you ever felt totally drained and rung out? David did. He felt like a pelican in the wilderness! Pelicans are at home in the water—not in the desert.

When we ignore sin, we banish ourselves to a spiritual desert. Our Christian lives dry up. We desperately need the forgiveness of Jesus Christ who said, "Whoever drinks of the water that I

57

shall give him will never thirst" (John 4:14).

In 2 Samuel, we read of David's adultery with Bathsheba. After he sinned with her, David refused to be honest with God about the wrong that he had done. He knew God's command: "Thou shalt not commit adultery." But he sinned anyway. And then he ignored his sin. The longer David waited to confess his sin, the deeper he fell.

When he discovered that Bathsheba was pregnant, he plotted to murder Uriah, her husband. So David violated God's will a second time. It took quite a while before David finally stopped ignoring his sin. And as he waited, things got worse.

For a while, David seemed to get away with it. But in God's moral universe, everyone reaps what he sows. And it should not surprise us that a series of tragedies followed David's sin. If you sow sexual freedom, you will reap its results. David's son Amnon picked up his father's bad habits. Amnon thought nothing of committing incest with his sister.

The same holds true today. The habits we form in our youth follow us. If we ignore our sin, these habits will be picked up by our children. If we live for the almighty dollar, our children will do so with fewer moral scruples than we did. If parents think nothing of adultery, they should not be surprised that their sons refer to homosexuality, incest, and kiddie porn as mere sexual preference.

## 2. CONFESSING SIN

Ignoring sin has deep consequences. Proverbs 28:13 states:

> He who covers his sins will not prosper,
> But whoever confesses and forsakes them will have
>   mercy.

Why should we confess our sins? The answer is simple. Our sin has separated us from God. We have chosen to run from His path. We have broken fellowship with Him. Adam and Eve did it on a colossal scale. We still do it today.

Confession is the foundation of forgiveness. It means honestly admitting to God that we are wrong and He is right. It means we acknowledge our need of deliverance from sin's power, that we need to be healed from sin's disease, that we need to be washed from sin's grime which accumulates around the human collar. In confession we admit that we need the Saviour.

Confession is prompted by a change of heart about sin. Scripture calls this change repentance. First John 1:9 tells us, "If we confess our sins, He is faithful and just to forgive us our sins and to cleanse us from all unrighteousness." Psalm 32:6 tells us, "Pray . . . in a time when [God] may be found." Then David adds, "Surely in a flood of great waters they shall not come near him." David suggests that we tend to wait until old age or a severe crisis before confessing our sins. "Don't wait!" he says. "Pray before the flood." When we wait we play games with Almighty God. By the time the flood came in Noah's day, the door of salvation was shut. The ark was sealed by God for the coming storm. Those outside perished.

Now is the day of grace. A day approaches when God will shut the door and issue His judgment. Confess your sins while God still extends His hand of grace and mercy.

But, you might ask, what if I'm not in church? Just as there is no better time than the present, there is no better place than the present place. Not only before the crisis, but whenever we slip back into sin we need to come to God. Since the Scriptures use words like "wash" and "cleanse" for salvation, we should have a clue as to how often we should confess. How often do we cleanse ourselves on a normal day? We take great care to brush our teeth, wash our hands, and to shower. Why? To get the dirt off that creeps into our lives. The same applies to confessing to God the sin in our lives and asking His cleansing.

A day starts out fresh. By 9 o'clock we have already had some choice words for several motorists or pedestrians. By noon we have slandered someone, lost our patience, or cut corners on expenses. By 3 P.M. we have lashed out verbally or grown lazy and cheated our employer by slowing down. By 5 o'clock we have unloaded on our spouse and the kids. By 6 o'clock we sit down for dinner and hear about the troubles of each family member. Later in the evening we take in the news to learn how badly the rest of the world has fared. Then we flop into bed, exhausted, needing rest. The next day we wake up and start the same routine over again.

Do you see how grimy our lives can become after five days of work? Do you see how essential it is to cleanse our lives each day in private and family worship, and then on Sunday in corporate worship? We need to confess our sins and place our trust where it ought to be.

## 3. FORGIVING SIN

Do you know what happens when we confess our sins? In Psalm 32, David discovered the joy of forgiveness. He wrote in verse 1: "Blessed [or happy] is he whose transgression is forgiven." The guilt is gone. The groaning stops. The vitality returns. A song comes to our lips. Verse 7 says, "You shall surround me with songs of deliverance."

Confession involves a change in the way we respond to God. Forgiveness involves a change in the way God responds to us.

Forgiveness has several meanings in Scripture. It can mean "to cover," "to take away," "to put aside," and "to pardon." When God forgives our sins, He sends them away. Psalm 103:12 says, "As far as the east is from the west, so far has He removed our transgressions from us."

How does forgiveness take place? In the Bible, forgiveness is always an expression of God's mercy extended to sinners. We receive this forgiveness when we repent and believe. However, the means of forgiveness differs in the Old and New Testaments.

In Old Testament times, God gave Israel a system of sacrifices to deal with sin. Offenders brought an unspotted animal to the altar at some cost to themselves. They would lay their hands on the animal, identifying with it in order to recognize it as a substitute. Then the animal was slain. The priest collected its blood and applied it to the altar. In this way, each offering provided a partial forgiveness for sin. The blood covered sins. There was an identification with the victim.

In New Testament times, God instituted the supreme way of dealing with sin. He Himself provided an offering at great cost. He sent His only Son, sinless as He was, to die on a cross. Jesus died in our place for our sins. His blood was an offering to God. It covered the offense of our sin once and for all. Most important, God's sacrifice did not have to be repeated, because Jesus overcame the power of death and rose from the grave.

What has all this to do with you? We no longer need to offer animal sacrifices every time we want to confess our sins. We need not worry about earning our salvation by our own works. Jesus' sacrifice was sufficient. Jesus paid the penalty for our sin. He stood in our place.

Not long ago a series of tornados devastated neighborhoods in eastern Ohio and western Pennsylvania. Nearly 100 people lost their lives. Before the storm, a man named David Kostka was umpiring a Little League baseball game in Wheatland, Pennsylvania. When David saw the black funnel bearing down on the field, he ran into the stands to grab his niece. He threw her into a ditch and covered her with his body. Then the tornado touched ground. When the little girl looked up, her uncle was gone. He became a victim of the deadly storm, but the life of his niece was saved. That's substitution.

In a similar way, Jesus placed His body where our bodies should have been. He stood in our place, taking our sins upon Himself so that we might live. By repenting of our sins and believing in what Jesus did for us on the cross, we can know complete forgiveness and deliverance from sin. For those who confess their sin, "the Lord does not impute iniquity" (Psalm 32:2). Rather, our sins are applied to Christ, and His life and righteousness are applied to us.

The most important confession you could ever make is to confess your sins to God. Recognize Jesus Christ as God's only provision for your sin. It is a major mistake to ignore your sin. It will not go away. It must be faced and confessed.

Christian friend, have you fallen back into old habits and kept silent about your sin? Confess your transgression to Jesus Christ who is rich in grace and ready to forgive all those who truly repent.

## REMEMBER

The psalmist tells us that sin and guilt can be covered and forgiven.

Confession means honestly admitting to God that we are wrong and He is right.

Confession involves a change in the way we respond to God. Forgiveness involves a change in the way God responds to us.

"As far as the east is from the west, so far has He removed our transgression from us" (Ps. 103:12).

# CHAPTER SEVEN

# GOD'S CURE FOR CARE

## PSALM 37

We are a nation of worriers! A panel of psychologists once concluded that 40 percent of what people worry about never happens. Thirty percent of worry is about events which have already taken place. Twelve percent has to do with needless concern over health. Ten percent deals with small trifles, and only 8 percent of what we worry about is related to legitimate concerns. If that is so, we surely waste a lot of time and energy worrying! Worry is not only emotionally draining, but it is a national health hazard.

During World War II, 300,000 Americans lost their lives in battle. And yet during the same time, over 2 million civilians died of heart disease. Medical authorities tell us that worry kills people. A fitting epitaph for many a tombstone could be, "Died of Worry." For many people, anxiety becomes a way of life—and death.

God's servant, David, knew a lot about the pressures of life. He was scorned by his brothers, envied by Saul, and even betrayed by his own son Absalom.

In Psalm 37 we have a picture of David trapped by his enemies. His situation appears hopeless, and yet he was able to say in verse 1, "Do not fret because of evildoers." The word *fret* means "to worry excessively."

Webster defines the word *fret* as "to cause to suffer emotional strain, or to eat or to gnaw into, to become uneasy, vexed or worried." In this beautiful psalm, David tells us, "Don't get into perilous heat over things." In the present vernacular, "Don't sweat it. Keep calm; hang loose."

When we worry, we reveal a basic distrust in God! The evildoers who surrounded David appeared to be doing well. They were the objects of envy. David sensed that some of his people had begun to look at the success of their enemies and become fretful.

In Psalm 73, the poet refers to the ungodly and being envious of their prosperity and wealth. It was causing him to be resentful and uneasy. He wrote that he could not understand this "until I went into the sanctuary of God; then I understood their end" (Psalm 73:17).

Always remember that the prosperity of the unbelieving lasts only for a time—not for eternity. They have their reward now, in this life. "They shall soon be cut down like the grass, and wither as the green herb" (Psalm 37:2). Their success is short-lived.

"Don't fret," David says. Fretting heats the bearings, but it rarely produces power. A hot axle always hinders progress: it never helps. In Psalm 37:1 David says, "Do not fret nor be envious of the workers of iniquity." Fretting and envy go hand in hand. Envy is a characteristic of earthly wisdom according to chapter 3 of James. It is difficult for us to stand by and see unbelievers, the ungodly, prosper. Envy and jealousy are wasted energy.

The zealous man and the jealous man are in a sense related, except that one is clean and the other is unclean. We need hot hearts, but never hot heads. We need zealous men and women, but not jealous men and women.

We need to pray with David in Psalm 51, "Create in me a clean heart, O God, and renew a steadfast spirit within me" (v. 10). In Psalm 37, David suggests five steps in the cure for care.

### 1. TRUST IN THE LORD (Psalm 37:3)

The word translated *trust* throughout the Old Testament means "without care," or literally, "careless" in its most pure form. To be careless, of course, does not mean flippant, but rather freedom from care. We find it pictured in the calm confidence of a little child at play knowing that his parents are present and he is safe. It is a positive trust and submission to the will of God.

The encouragement of I Peter 5:7 is for "casting all your care upon Him, for He cares for you."

J.B. Phillips renders the Apostle Paul's words to the Philippians (4:6-7) this way:

> Don't worry over anything whatever; tell God every detail of your needs in earnest and thankful prayer, and the peace of God, which transcends human understanding, will keep constant guard over your hearts and minds as they rest in Christ Jesus.

The first step, then, in God's cure for care is to trust in the Lord.

### 2. DO GOOD (Psalm 37:3)

"Trust in the Lord, and do good." Doing good is a superb cure for worry; it is a wholesome and holy activity. Work is healthy. Work seldom kills people—worry does!

If you are smothered by care, I encourage you to become genuinely interested in others. I have seen many more people helped by accepting responsibility and becoming involved in the needs of others than by anything else.

When was the last time you took care of a tired mother's children so that she could go shopping? When did you last invite a student or a serviceman to your home for dinner? How long has it been since you offered to do some chore for one of the elderly?

Why not determine to do good today to help someone? One of the best cures for worry is wholesome activity. David said, "Trust in the Lord, and do good." Do something for someone, because everyone you meet is carrying a burden.

### 3. DELIGHT YOURSELF IN THE LORD (Psalm 37:4)

Literally, David is saying, "Seek for the delicacies that are to be found in knowing the Lord. Learn of His wisdom, His power, His compassion." Do you really know Him and enjoy Him? Verse 4 continues: "And He shall give you the desires of your heart."

Now you ask, "Does the Lord really give us the desires of our hearts?" I believe He does. In 1 Kings 3 the Lord asked King Solomon what he wanted. Solomon answered, wisdom. God gave Solomon wisdom, plus riches and honor. On the road to Jericho, Jesus asked blind Bartimeus, "What do you want Me to do for you?" Bartimeus replied, "That I may receive my sight" (Mark 10:46-52). And his sight was restored. The dying thief on the cross said to Jesus, "Remember me when You come into Your kingdom." And Jesus said, "Today you will be with Me in Paradise" (Luke 23:39-43).

God is generous. David says in Psalm 23, "My cup runs over" (v. 5). The Apostle James says, "Ask of God, who gives to all liberally" (James 1:5). God wants to do more for us than we could even imagine. If we sincerely and completely delight ourselves in Him, He will give us the desires of our hearts.

When we worry, we put the uncertain cloud of tomorrow over the glorious sunshine of today. Many people worry so much about the needs of the next day, week, or year that they fail to enjoy the provision God has made for them today. Live today enjoying God's presence. Someone has written a humorous little poem that says:

> The worried cow would have lived till now,
>   If she had saved her breath;
> But she feared her hay wouldn't last all day,
>   And she mooed herself to death.

Do you know people like that? Many people are "mooing" themselves to death in their constant worry over material things. Jesus said in Matthew 6:34, "Do not worry about tomorrow, for tomorrow will worry about its own things. Sufficient for the day is its own trouble." The load of tomorrow added to the burden of today is enough to make even the strongest fail. We need to shut off the future just as tightly as we shut off the past! Consider this thought from W.J. Jeffers' book *New Horizons*:

> There are two days in the week about which I never worry—yesterday and tomorrow. Yesterday, with its mistakes and blunders, has passed forever beyond recall. I cannot undo any act that I wrought. I cannot unsay a word that I said. All that it holds of my life—of wrongs, regret, and sorrow—is in the hands of God who can bring honey out of the rock, turn weeping into laughter, and give beauty for ashes.

> Tomorrow, with all its possible adversities, burdens, failures, and mistakes is as far beyond my reach as its dead sister—yesterday.

> There is left for me but one day of the week—today. Any man can fight the battles of today. Anyone can resist the temptations of today. It is when we willfully add the burden of yesterday and tomorrow that we break down. Only God can sustain such burdens. In

infinite wisdom, He has carefully measured out to us our day's portion, and He gives the promise, "As your days, so shall your strength be" (Deut. 33:25).

## 4. COMMIT YOUR WAY TO THE LORD (Psalm 37:5)

"Commit your way to the Lord, trust also in Him, and He shall bring it to pass." In other words, put God in charge of your life. Let Him have complete control. Cast all your burdens and opportunities upon Him, and He will bring you peace of heart and soul.

Mental disorganization figures as one of the chief factors in worry. The helter-skelter mind is always weary and overburdened. Deferred decisions have a way of adding up when they are not dealt with. And if they are ignored long enough, they will eventually swamp you. David is saying, "Stop trying to run your own life!" Let the Lord have control.

The questions today are: Have you committed yourself to Jesus Christ? Are you going forward or backward? Are you for Jesus or against Him?

Remember, you cannot commit your way unto Him until you have received Christ as your personal Saviour and Lord.

Is your life burdened by care? Is there something troubling you deep inside? The Bible says, "Trust, delight, and commit yourself to Him.

## 5. REST IN THE LORD (Psalm 37:7)

Matthew records the gracious invitation of Jesus:

> Come to Me, all you who labor and are heavy laden, and I will give you rest. Take My yoke upon you and learn from Me, for I am gentle and lowly in heart, and you will find rest for your souls (11:28-29).

First there is the "rest" of receiving Jesus Christ. Then there is the rest of becoming a partner with God. Accept His yoke.

Trust Him. Delight in Him. Commit your way unto Him, and you will experience a rest beyond anything you could imagine.

Don't forget, God is *for* you. He is not neutral concerning you. He loves you and wants to be the answer to all your care. In an act of faith and trust, commit yourself and your worries to the Lord right now.

## REMEMBER

When we worry, we reveal a basic distrust in God!

"Don't worry over anything whatever; tell God every detail of your needs in earnest and thankful prayer, and the peace of God, which transcends human understanding, will keep constant guard over your hearts and minds as they rest in Christ Jesus" (Phil. 4:6-7, PH).

Work seldom kills people—worry does!

God wants to do more for us than we could even imagine.

Cast all your burdens and opportunities upon Him and He will bring you peace of heart and soul.

God is too wise to make a mistake, and too loving to be unkind.

# CHAPTER EIGHT

# SOMETHING TO SING ABOUT

## PSALM 40

Popular humorist Erma Bombeck once wrote a book titled *If Life Is a Bowl of Cherries, What Am I Doing in the Pits?* Life, for thousands of people, is the pits! In spite of greater opportunities for leisure, many people simply endure life rather than enjoy it.

Shakespeare described life as "a tale told by a fool . . . full of sound and fury and signifying nothing." There is no doubt about it—life for some is a broken record, going in circles, playing the same old melody.

Two graduates of Moody Bible Institute from the class of 1946, John and Elaine Beekman, gave themselves to serve the Lord among the Chol Indians of southern Mexico. They rode mules, traveled the waterways in dugout canoes, and with others toiled for over twenty-five years to translate the entire New Testament into the Chol Indian language.

The church in Chol country now thrives—a strong, evangelistic fellowship of well over 12,000 believers, and they fully support themselves. The Chol Indians as a people were never known to have sung. But with the coming of the Gospel, the believers became known as "the singers." They love to sing because now they have something to sing about.

Psalm 40 tells us about David and the reason for his song. Notice the first three verses:

> I waited patiently for the Lord;
> And He inclined to me,
> And heard my cry.
> He also brought me up out of a horrible pit,
> Out of the miry clay,
> And set my feet upon a rock,
> And established my steps.
> He has put a new song in my mouth—
> Praise to our God;
> Many will see it and fear,
> And will trust in the Lord.

David does not reveal the nature of his horrible pit. It may have been physical sickness. Maybe it was persecution, slander, or maybe adultery that caused him to sink in the miry clay. But David called to the Lord, and the Lord heard him, and delivered him from his condition of despair.

## 1. THE SOURCE OF DAVID'S SONG

David was not singing just by chance, neither did he sing because he was young and strong. Many young people today have little to sing about. One of the songs made popular almost twenty-five years ago by the Beatles echoes this condition, declaring that "yesterday all my troubles seemed so far away . . . [but] now it seems as though they are here to stay." The song goes on to describe the futility of today and the emptiness of tomorrow. Anything worthwhile, according to the song, is past and gone.

Undoubtedly, one of the reasons this song by the Beatles

became so popular is its portrayal of the emptiness and hope-lessness felt by a large segment of society. What is there to live for when one leaves God out of the picture? Today is nothing and tomorrow holds no hope. But David's song in Psalm 40 was not at all like that. Rather than living with past memories, David deals with the here and now in this psalm.

Nor was David able to sing because of great prosperity. Actually, he was not prosperous at all at this point in time. David had little in the way of material possessions. Neither did he sing simply because of rugged determination—the attitude of "I'm going to sing if it kills me."

There are some songs which suggest that the answer to trouble is to "put on a happy face." In fact, one of the old songs of the past says, "Pack up your troubles in your old kit bag, and smile, smile, smile!" A later tune suggests, "Smile, though your heart is aching; smile, though it's nearly breaking. . . . Just smile, smile, smile."

No, David did not sing just to psych himself up. David had a reason to sing. The source of David's song was God Himself. Psalm 40:3 reads, "He put a new song in my mouth."

The Good News of Jesus Christ and singing are inseparable. By contrast, unbelief has few songs or anthems. Atheism is songless. When the renowned infidel Robert Ingersol died, the funeral program read, "There will be no singing." Of course not! Singing, for the most part, is related to a feeling of warmth and well-being.

When Jesus was born, Luke tells us, "And suddenly there was with the angel a multitude of the heavenly host praising God!" (2:13). And when a sinner is converted to Jesus Christ, the Bible says heaven rejoices (Luke 15:7).

Revelation 19:6 describes great praise and joy when Christ returns to reign:

> And I heard, as it were, the voice of a great multi-tude, as the sound of many waters and as the sound

of mighty thunders, saying, "Alleluia! For the Lord God Omnipotent reigns! Let us be glad and rejoice and give Him glory, for the marriage of the Lamb has come."

All of us at times in our lives run out of courage. But when you know that the Lord is your light and your salvation, then you can say with the psalmist, "Whom shall I fear?" (Ps. 27:1). We all lack strength. But with the Apostle Paul, we who know Christ can say, "I can do all things through Christ who strengthens me" (Phil. 4:13). Jesus Christ makes all the difference.

Each of us needs wisdom, and we who know the Saviour can claim the promise of the Bible: "If any of you lacks wisdom, let him ask of God, who gives to all liberally" (James 1:5). My friend, for every need you have, a corresponding fullness for that need is found in the person of Jesus Christ. Yes, the source of David's song was God Himself.

Salvation and song are twins. There was a time in the history of the nation Israel when the temple, the symbol of the moral stature of the people, was in total disarray. Everything had been allowed to deteriorate. Even the Word of God was lost in the rubbish that filled the temple. It was the kind of spiritual decay that we see in some circles today.

But a very interesting thing happened. Under the leadership of good King Josiah, the people caught a brand-new vision. They repaired the temple. The ordinances of the Law were revived. The Word of God was restored to its rightful place. And then, 2 Chronicles 35:15 tells us that "the singers . . . were in their places," and the house of the Lord was filled again with glorious music in praise to God.

You see, the joy of the Lord produces music in the soul. And when people are right and in tune with God, they have to sing. It was that way when Martin Luther translated the Bible into the language of the people. Soon all of Europe started to sing:

A mighty fortress is our God,
    A bulwark never failing;
Our helper He, amid the flood
    Of mortal ills prevailing.
For still our ancient foe
    Doth seek to work us woe;
His craft and power are great,
    And armed with cruel hate,
On earth is not his equal.

The Apostle Paul told the church at Ephesus to praise God by "speaking to one another in psalms and hymns and spiritual songs, singing and making melody in your heart to the Lord" (Eph. 5:19). The psalmist wrote, "I will sing of the mercies of the Lord forever; with my mouth will I make known Your faithfulness to all generations" (Ps. 89:1). Never forget it—God is the source of our song. And the song that God gives is a lasting song.

Furthermore, the song that God gives does not change. Oh, there are changes all about us. There is change in the relations of men to God, but there is no change in Him. His being never changes. His attributes never change. There is no change in His purposes. His promises never change. There is no change in His song. The Gospel chorus of "In My Heart There Rings a Melody" says, " 'Twill be my endless theme in glory, with the angels I will sing."

Hymnwriter Henry Lyte leads us to sing, "Change and decay in all around I see; O Thou who changest not, abide with me." And we sing A.B. Simpson's "Yesterday, today, forever—Jesus is the same. All may change, but Jesus never, glory to His name!" The Apostle James put it this way in James 1:17: "Every good gift and every perfect gift is from above, and comes down from the Father of lights, with whom there is no variation or shadow of turning." The unchanging, triune God is the source of our divine song. Our great God was the source of David's song, and He is the source for the song of all those who trust in Christ.

## 2. THE REASON FOR DAVID'S SONG

Psalm 40:2 reads: "He also brought me up out of a horrible pit, out of the miry clay, and set my feet upon a rock, and established my steps."

David said that the place from which God had rescued him was "a horrible pit." Now, David does not explain exactly what he meant by that, but we know it must have been a trying situation—perhaps like the situation you find yourself in right now. Then David called for help, and the Lord heard him and came to his aid. It was probably like the experience of songwriter James Rowe who wrote:

> I was sinking deep in sin,
>     Far from the peaceful shore,
> Very deeply stained within,
>     Sinking to rise no more;
> But the Master of the sea
>     Heard my despairing cry,
> From the waters lifted me,
>     Now safe am I.

Do you know God's saving power? Have you experienced God's delivering power? Perhaps you too find yourself in sin's tenacious grip. Possibly you are a slave to lust, or obsessed with worldly possessions. But you can be changed. You can experience God's power right where you are.

David's song was a song of deliverance. But more, it was a song of confidence. "He [the Lord] has set my feet upon a rock and established my steps." Once David floundered, but now we see him stable, confident in the Lord. His feet are on the rock. David's foundation is sure. He could stand tall and sing because he was resting in the Lord. He could say, "Though I walk through the valley of the shadow of death, I will fear no evil; for You are with me" (Ps. 23:4).

Someone might ask, "Why sing?" Because all nature sings. If we are silent, then we are the exception to God's creation. The thunder praises Him as it rolls like many drums. The rain sings softly as it falls in the springtime. The ocean seems to sing and praise Him as it claps against the shore. The mountains and the woods have their distinctive song. How shall we—men and women for whom the stars and sun were created—how shall we not sing? We cannot help but sing.

There is another reason for possessing a song in our hearts. Psalm 40:3 says, "Many will see it and fear, and will trust in the Lord." See what? See a song? Did David use the wrong word here? Should he not have said, "Many shall hear it?" No, he meant, "Many shall *see* it."

David's new song echoed his life. David had become a song. The person who possesses the new song of the Gospel will display it in every aspect of life. Yes, many shall see it.

As a teenager, I enjoyed—and still enjoy—the Gospel song "In My Heart There Rings a Melody" by Elton M. Roth that I mentioned earlier:

> I have a song that Jesus gave me,
>     It was sent from heaven above;
> There never was a sweeter melody,
>     'Tis a melody of love.
>
> I love the Christ who died on Calvary,
>     For He washed my sins away;
> He put within my heart a melody,
>     And I know it's there to stay.
>
> 'Twill be my endless theme in glory,
>     With the angels I will sing;
> 'Twill be a song with glorious harmony,
>     When the courts of heaven ring.

# SOMETHING TO SING ABOUT

In my heart there rings a melody,
   There rings a melody with heaven's harmony;
In my heart there rings a melody,
   There rings a melody of love. *

The gift of God, eternal life through Jesus Christ, is something to sing about!

## REMEMBER

The Good News of Jesus Christ and singing are inseparable.

For every need you have, a corresponding fullness for that need is found in the person of Jesus Christ.

The joy of the Lord produces music in the soul.

God is the source of our song. The song that God gives is a lasting song.

# CHAPTER NINE

# THE JOY OF FORGIVENESS

## PSALM 51

S ome time ago, while waiting to board a plane at Chicago's O'Hare International Airport, I spoke with a doctor and his wife. After watching several planes thunder down the runway and jet off into the fog, the wife said, "I wish I could vanish into space just like that plane. I'd like to escape and go somewhere and start my life all over again."

She was young and attractive, obviously a woman of means, and yet she wanted to get away from it all. Why? Why did she want to vanish? Why did she want to escape? Because the stained hand of the past was reaching into the present and making life unlivable.

Many people today echo this same despair. Millions of people are driven by the haunting desire to escape. And while some want to escape, others look for something to help them drop out. Some turn to alcohol to drown their fears. Others escape through drugs. Still others turn to sex or a career or the making of money—anything to help them forget life's situations.

Why do so many in our world seek an escape? Because they do

not know about the restoration that God offers—"the joy of forgiveness."

Just suppose we could sin but not repent. Suppose God would allow us to fall with no possibility of getting up. Suppose we were able to wander from God but were unable to return to God.

It is the truth of repentance that provides hope for the world. The lost can be found. The fallen can be lifted. The wayward can be restored. The sinner can be saved.

Unquestionably, scores of people know nothing of the forgiveness found in the Gospel. They have never trusted Christ as Saviour. The Bible describes them as "dead in trespasses and sins" (Eph. 2:1). They are dead to the joys God offers; dead to the pardon He makes available.

Then there are others who go by the name of Christian, who are saved, yet so as by fire. They live with unconfessed sin, sin that chokes out the reality and vitality of their life in Christ.

Israel's King David, though versatile and extremely talented, sinned greatly. In 2 Samuel 11-12 read how David committed adultery with Bathsheba, the wife of Uriah. Then later he arranged to have Uriah killed on the battlefield. This tragic deed totally offended God.

Nathan, God's prophet, came to David to confront him. Tactfully, Nathan told David a story of a rich man who had great possessions. This man took the only lamb of a poor man to prepare a welcome feast for a visiting friend.

David had been a shepherd boy and without doubt had a pet lamb from time to time. When King David heard this story of injustice, he was angry. With great indignation he said, "As the Lord lives, the man who has done this shall surely die!" Nathan courageously pointed his finger at David and said, "You are the man!" He used this story to tell David that he had taken Bathsheba, Uriah's "pet lamb."

Psalm 51 pictures David overwhelmed with guilt. Convicted by the voice of God, he cried out in despair. He saw himself as he actually was, and what he saw he did not like. Under this great weight of guilt, David pleaded to God for mercy. Psalm 51 is David's prayer of repentance. He called out to the Lord for forgiveness—and miracle of miracles—God heard and answered his prayer.

In a psalm probably written later, David describes the joy of the person "whose transgression is forgiven, whose sin is covered" (Psalm 32:1). But how did this happen? How did David get back into fellowship with God? How did he come to experience the joy of forgiveness? And, knowing that, what can we learn from David's experience that will help us find the same joy?

Each of us, regardless of who we are, stands where David stood. The Bible tells us that if we look with lust, we are guilty. No person is innocent before the Holy God. But the good news is, we can know God's forgiveness. We do not have to be separated from fellowship with God. We can enjoy walking with Him once again.

For at least a year, David lived in anguish apart from fellowship with God. He suffered deeply until he confessed his sin and experienced the joy of forgiveness. Psalm 51 gives four steps leading to the joy of forgiveness.

## 1. DAVID ADMITTED HIS SIN AND PRAYED FOR PARDON

This penitential psalm is remarkable because it does not contain one word of excuse. Like an erupting volcano sending out its lava, David cries out to the Lord for mercy and pardon. He realizes his need for help. David makes no excuses. Neither does he remind God of all his mighty acts of valor or of his great leadership of the people. He simply and honestly says, "I'm guilty, and I need forgiveness."

David also acknowledged the personal character of his sin. Notice verse 1 where he says, "Blot out my transgressions." Verse 2 says, "Wash me thoroughly from my iniquity, and cleanse me from my sin." David speaks of himself thirty-three times in this psalm. He does not try to blame his sin on circumstances, or his temperament, or on human weakness. All of these factors may have played a part in David's sin. But his conscience told him that he alone was guilty before the holy God.

Oftentimes we find it easy to confess the sins of others, or the sins of the church, or the sins of the nation. However, we find it very difficult to come before God and say, "I am guilty. I have sinned. I'm the one." Notice Psalm 51:3: "For I acknowledge my transgressions, and my sin is ever before me."

Conscious awareness of sin must be the instigator of any prayer of forgiveness. Not just shame at being discovered or even sorrow over the evil results, but a deep realization that I stand guilty and condemned before the holy God.

The first words David spoke following Nathan's stinging pronouncement were, "I have sinned against the Lord." He stood guilty before God, and he knew it. Realization of our personal guilt must always come before we can experience the joy of forgiveness.

Not only did David realize his guilt, but he also realized that his sin was directed against God. David confessed, "Against You, You only, have I sinned, and done this evil in Your sight" (v. 4).

Sin, regardless of its nature, transcends the human relation. It reaches to the very throne of heaven. It is against God Himself. But what about Bathsheba? You ask, "Wasn't she defiled? And Uriah, wasn't he murdered? Surely David's sin was committed against these people as well."

Yes, David's sin was directed toward Uriah and Bathsheba, but it was also committed against God. God is the ultimate reality; and because David sinned against God, it was from Him that he had to seek forgiveness.

My friend, never forget that important point. When we sin against others, or when we take advantage of someone, we

81

defile the very person of God Himself. So, as step number 1, David admitted his sin and prayed for pardon.

## 2. DAVID ASKED FOR PERSONAL CLEANSING
Psalm 51:7 reads:

Purge me with hyssop and I shall be clean;
Wash me, and I shall be whiter than snow.

The picture here is not a superficial rinsing, but a thorough and repeated scrubbing, a complete cleansing from the pollution and power of sin. When God washes, He washes clean! Madison Avenue bombards us with the claims of laundry detergents that go deep down and get out ground-in dirt. But the small print informs us that "no cleaning agent can remove all stains." The blood of Christ can clean deep down. And it gets out the most stubborn of moral stains. The answer to David's problem and our problem is this divine cleansing.

The Prophet Isaiah tells us that even our righteousness is as a filthy rag in the sight of a Holy God. David acknowledged his need for a total overhaul, a complete spiritual bath to rid him of the impact of sin:

Behold, You desire truth in the inward parts,
And in the hidden part You will
make me to know wisdom (v. 6).

Often we want to wash our hands and face, so that we appear clean, but we do not want to allow God to cleanse us completely in the inward parts. We want a whitewash but not that "washing white" which makes us pure as new fallen snow. God calls for total cleansing.

Out of the depths of his utter hopelessness, David cries in verse 10, "Create in me a clean heart, O God, and renew a steadfast spirit within me."

In the days of his youth, David had been strong. He accomplished great things for God. But his sin shattered his confidence. Communication was broken with the Heavenly Father, and David needed total renewal.

Has this been your experience? Do you need renewal? Just like David, you can come back. You can know the joy of personal cleansing and personal pardon.

## 3. DAVID PRAYED FOR RESTORATION AND THE JOY OF SALVATION

In Psalm 51:12, David asks of God: "Restore to me the joy of Your salvation." In other words, he asks that God will let him know again the peace and rest that he once knew. The word *joy* speaks of exaltation, a happy exuberant feeling. It is a state of contentment with God and all that He has done in one's life. God desires His children to have this peace and joy. But it is a peace and joy which comes only through complete fellowship with Him. God longs to give back the joy of salvation to all those who have lost it.

David experienced the effect of sin in his life. He watched as his life became a meaningless existence. Then he prayed for restoration. Perhaps you have lost the joy of your salvation, and you are missing the peace of mind only God can give. Pray, as David did, and ask His forgiveness.

## 4. DAVID REDEDICATED HIMSELF TO THE SERVICE OF GOD

In Psalm 51:13-15, David told God,

> Then I will teach transgressors Your ways,
> And sinners shall be converted to You. . . .
> And my tongue shall sing aloud of
>     Your righteousness. . . .
> And my mouth shall show forth Your praise.

After coming before God in confession and repentance, David renewed his vows to God. Already knowing the joy of forgiveness, he longed to do something about it. He wanted to tell others the good news of God's mercy. He said, "I will teach." He said, "My tongue shall sing." He said, "My mouth shall show forth Thy praise."

Those who realize the greatness of sin and who understand the greatness of God's forgiveness are compelled to tell others of the joy of sins forgiven. They cannot keep quiet!

What about you? Are you bogged down by sin? Are you living a defeated life? Have you lost the joy of salvation? God's forgiveness is just as available to you as it was to David. If you seek it, God will revolutionize your life.

However, God does not force His forgiveness on anyone. He waits for us to respond, for us to ask, for us to seek His forgiveness. He provided a means for that forgiveness on an ancient Roman cross. Now He anxiously awaits to apply it to the lives of His children. Yet, he will not do so until we recognize our sin and seek His forgiveness. Then He will restore unto us the joy of His salvation.

Perhaps you have never committed your life to Christ. Right now you can experience the joy of forgiveness. You can come to know salvation. You may say, "I haven't committed murder. I haven't committed adultery. I'm not a bad person."

The Bible says that no matter who you are, or what you have or have not done, you stand guilty before a holy God. All men are sinners. None of us measures up to God's standards of holiness. All must repent. If you have not done so, come to Christ today. Acknowledge your guilt. Seek His cleansing, and experience the joy of forgiveness.

## REMEMBER

Conscious awareness of sin must be the instigator of any prayer of forgiveness.

Sin, regardless of its nature, transcends the human relation.

It reaches to the very throne of heaven. It is against God Himself.

God's forgiveness is not a superficial rinsing, but a thorough and repeated scrubbing, a complete cleansing from the pollution and power of sin.

God desires His children to have that peace and joy which only results from complete fellowship with Him.

Those who realize the greatness of sin and who understand the greatness of God's forgiveness are compelled to tell others of sins forgiven.

God does not force His forgiveness on anyone.

CHAPTER TEN

# A TIME FOR TEARS

1 Samuel 21: 10-15

## PSALM 56

The he Old Testament Book of Ecclesiastes contains an
interesting concept:

To everything there is a season,
A time for every purpose under heaven:
A time to be born,
And a time to die;
A time to plant,
And a time to pluck what is planted;
A time to kill,
And a time to heal;
A time to break down,
And a time to build up;
A time to weep,
And a time to laugh;
A time to mourn,
And a time to dance (3:1-4).

I have a longtime friend with whom I occasionally talk. One day he told me that one of his neighbors died. I asked, "Was your neighbor your friend?" "No," he said, "we never cried together."

My old friend felt that shedding tears together spoke of a special bond and intimacy. And you know, he is right.

The shortest verse in the Bible consists of only two words: "Jesus wept" (John 11:35). The tears of Jesus communicated something of His deep love and compassion for Lazarus, Mary, and Martha. There is a time to weep and a time to mourn. Tears are the silent language of sorrow.

Psalm 56 speaks of the tears of David: "My enemies would hound me all day, for there are many who fight against me" (v. 2). / "All day they twist my words; all their thoughts are against me for evil" (v. 5). / "They gather together, they hide, they mark my steps when they lie in wait for my life" (v. 6). / "You number my wanderings; put my tears into Your bottle; are they not in Your book?" (v. 8)

In Bible times it was customary for each family to own a "tear bottle." The tear bottle represented all the heartaches of life. It was with a tear bottle that Mary washed the feet of Jesus. Luke indicates that Jesus was deeply moved by her act of love and devotion, because the woman's tears represented all her failure, sins, and heartaches.

Each of us experiences his or her own heartaches. Sorrows come to everyone. But what a comfort to remember that the God who knows the flight of the sparrow, the God who dresses the flowers of the field, the God who paints the sunset knows and cares about your tears. He cares about you!

The Bible mentions different kinds of tears. As you meditate on Psalm 56, think also of these various kinds of tears described in Scripture.

## 1. THE TEARS OF LONELINESS
Genesis 21 speaks about the tears of loneliness:

So Abraham rose early in the morning, and took bread and a skin of water; and putting it on her shoulder, he gave it and the boy to Hagar, and sent her away. Then she departed and wandered in the Wilderness of Beersheba. And the water in the skin was used up, and she placed the boy under one of the shrubs. Then she went and sat down across from him at a distance of about a bowshot; for she said to herself, "Let me not see the death of the boy." So she sat opposite him, and lifted her voice and wept (vv. 14-16).

Can you see the picture? God had promised Abraham that he would be the father of a great nation. But despite this promise, Sarah, his wife, remained without children. After many years of waiting, and at the suggestion of Sarah, Abraham took Hagar, Sarah's handmaiden, who bare him a son, Ishmael.

Sarah, in a fit of jealousy, insisted that Hagar and her son be expelled from Abraham's home. And so Hagar and her child were cast out into the wilderness with no home, no husband, and very limited provisions!

Overcome with utter despair, Hagar placed her failing son under some shrubs and wandered away to cry. The Bible says, "She lifted up her voice and wept" (Gen. 21:16). Oh, the tears of loneliness!

The poet has captured something of the depth of despondency that is experienced by lonely people:

What purest delights are nipt in the blossom,
When those we love best are laid low.
When grief plants in secret her thorn in the bosom,
Deserted—to whom shall we go?

When with error bewildered our path becomes dreary,
And tears of despondence flow.

When the whole head is sick and the whole heart is
  weary,
Despairing—to whom shall we go?

The answer is that the Lord our God understands and cares
and wants to make a difference.

Lee Harvey Oswald, the man who killed President John F.
Kennedy, was a loner. His father died before he was born. He
was never close to his mother, who had to work at a number of
jobs in order to support her family.

One of Oswald's teachers remembers him as a poor student,
one who was "an introvert . . . a loner." At seventeen he quit
high school and joined the Marines. Twice he faced court-
martial for violating regulations. A man who served with him
recalls, "He was a lonely, introverted man."

Another man, who lived in the same rooming house as Oswald, said, "I didn't know him by name. Everybody left him
alone."

This world is filled with lonely people. Throngs of people
living alone in our metropolitan areas are lonely. The elderly
who have been pushed aside and often forgotten experience
loneliness. The corporation executive, the welfare recipient,
the Hollywood star, the student on a large university campus,
all feel lonely. Loneliness is no respecter of position or status in
life.

Dante, in one of his poems, writes, "At the midpoint of my
life I came to the Dark Wood." Do you know where the Dark
Wood is? It is the time when enthusiasm fades, the zest for life
runs out, and the tears of loneliness flow.

Richard Wolff in his book *The Meaning of Loneliness* says:

> Loneliness is universal because man is linked to God,
> his Creator, but disregards Him in his daily life. In
> this sense, loneliness is only an elementary expression
> of original sin. Sin is divisive, separates from God; sin

cancels the divine glory in man and deceives. Substitutions are attempted but human glory can never meet man's deepest need.

Even for true believers, a degree of loneliness is normal and to be expected. Hebrews 11:13 calls Old Testament believers "strangers and pilgrims on earth." "This world is not my home, I'm just a-passing through," says the familiar song. Life here is incomplete, and we long for our eternal home. But the promises of God give us comfort and calm our lonely spirits.

For the person without Jesus Christ, however, there is often little cure for the tears of loneliness.

The Lord Jesus knew what it was like to be lonely. In whatever form your loneliness might take, Jesus experienced that.

Perhaps you are poor. Jesus was so poor that He was born in a stable among cattle and buried in a borrowed tomb.

Perhaps you have never been given respect as a person. Jesus was a refugee whose civil rights often were denied.

Perhaps you have been falsely accused. Jesus was called a drunkard simply because He was trying to help those in need.

Jesus knew what it was like to be lonely. In the Garden of Gethsemane, He prayed all alone. On the cross He called out, "My God, My God, why have You forsaken Me?" (Matt. 27:46; Mark 15:34). Jesus sat where you sit. He felt unwanted. He felt rejection. He felt deep loneliness.

In Genesis 21, God called out to Hagar and brought her out of her seemingly impossible situation. God heard David in Psalm 56:9 when David said, "When I cry out to You, then my enemies will turn back; this I know, because God is for me." "God is for me." That brings comfort to the lonely heart.

## 2. THE TEARS OF DESOLATION

God's Prophet Jeremiah writes:

Oh, that my head were waters,

And my eyes a fountain of tears,
That I might weep day and night
For the slain of the daughter of my people! (9:1)

And in Jeremiah 9:18 he writes:

Let them make haste
And take up a wailing for us,
That our eyes may run with tears,
And our eyelids gush with water.

In 931 B.C., following the reign of King Solomon, the people of Israel were divided into the Northern and Southern Kingdoms. Jeroboam sat on the throne in the North with its capital at Samaria. Rehoboam ruled the South with its capital at Jerusalem. Sensing the evil and confusion of his time, Isaiah denounced the religious formality of the people. Their worship had become mechanical. They were honoring God with their lips and not with their hearts. Isaiah begged the people to repent, but they would not. As a result, God allowed the Assyrians to crush Samaria underfoot. The people were taken captive and the destruction was beyond description.

Jeremiah walked the streets of Jerusalem calling, "Repent," but the people would not listen to his words. Despite his many warnings, the same fate awaited the Southern Kingdom. By the year 587 B.C., all of Jerusalem was leveled to the ground. The temple was destroyed, homes were burned, and many people perished. Nothing remained but blood, death, and tears. The tears of desolation.

Four times I toured Europe after World War II and saw sheer desolation. I walked through refugee camps and listened to one tragedy after another. I looked into haunted eyes and saw and felt the tears of desolation.

In 1980, I saw desolation in Thailand and Cambodia among the refugees of Asia.

More recently, through the newspapers and television accounts, we witnessed in Mexico City the tears and anguish of many who lost their loved ones in an earthquake—tears of desolation

## 3. TEARS OF LOVING SERVICE

The Apostle Paul expressed his soul when he wrote to the Corinthian Christians: "Out of much affliction and anguish of heart I wrote to you, with many tears" (2 Cor. 2:4). Paul served the Lord "with many tears." He felt deep hurts of people.

Notice the words he uses when writing to the Romans: "For I could wish that I myself were accursed from Christ for my brethren, my kinsman according to the flesh" (9:3). Paul served night and day with tears.

Consider the tears of Jesus over Jerusalem: "How often I wanted to gather your children together, as a hen gathers her chicks under her wings, but you were not willing!" (Matt. 23:37) Jesus shed tears for a city. He served with tears.

The story is told of a young Salvation Army officer who found his work in a certain city just about impossible. Discouraged and defeated, the young man sent a wire to General Booth which read, "Have tried everything, am ready to quit." General Booth wired back: "Try tears." The tears of compassionate service.

Do you know anything about tears of compassion, the tears of service? Can you say with David, "Put my tears into Your bottle; are they not in Your book?" (Ps. 56:8) God records our tears; our sorrows He enters in His book.

## 4. THE TEARS OF REPENTANCE

The Gospels tell how Mary washed the feet of Jesus with tears of sorrow and repentance. Mary's tears spoke of her heart's desire for God's mercy and forgiveness. She abhorred her past sins. Have you experienced the tears of repentance?

Matthew 26:75 tells about Peter after his denial of Jesus:

"And Peter remembered the word of Jesus who had said to him, 'Before the rooster crows, you will deny Me three times.' Then he went out and wept bitterly." Peter shed meaningful tears of repentance.

Paul told the Corinthians:

> Now I rejoice, not that you were made sorry, but that your sorrow led to repentance. For you were made sorry in a godly manner, that you might suffer loss from us in nothing. For godly sorrow produces repentance to salvation, not to be regretted; but the sorrow of the world produces death (2 Cor. 7:9-10).

Have you come to Jesus Christ with tears of repentance? Have you sought His forgiveness? Have you placed your faith in Jesus Christ alone? Have you experienced the tears of repentance?

From the Garden of Eden until now, tears have fallen. But there is a day coming when the God who collects our tears will wipe all tears from our eyes (Rev. 7:18). There will be no tears tomorrow. No more tears, no more pain, no more death—but life eternal.

God cares about you. You may be a number to the Social Security Administration or to the telephone company, but you are a loved person to God. Not a sparrow falls that He does not see. He wants to be your Saviour and friend.

## REMEMBER

What a comfort to remember that the God who knows the flight of the sparrow, the God who dresses the flowers of the field, and the God who paints the sunset knows and cares about your tears.

Loneliness is no respecter of position or status in life.

It is the promises of God which give us comfort and calm our lonely spirit.

Not a sparrow falls that He does not see. He wants to be your Saviour and friend.

# CHAPTER ELEVEN

# THE REAL YOU

## PSALM 66

P salm 66 is a song of thanksgiving. Once again in celebration of deliverance, the psalmist calls upon all the
earth to praise God in verses 1-12. Then, in verses 18-
19, he encourages the people to pray:

> If I regard iniquity in my heart,
> The Lord will not hear.
> But certainly God has heard me;
> He has attended to the voice of my prayer.

Repairing the underground of a city is a never-ending job. In
fact, the underground with its water lines, sewers, and electric-
ity is the real heart of a city. Without the underground, all the
buildings are dark and dead.

As the Prophet Samuel searched out a new king for Israel, he
came to one of the sons of Jesse named Eliab. He was striking
in outward appearance, but the Scripture reads:

Do not look at his appearance or at the height of his stature, because I have refused him. For the Lord does not see as man sees; for man looks at the outward appearance, but the Lord looks at the heart (1 Sam. 16:7).

Always remember that God sees beyond the externals to the real you. God looks not at the skyline of your life, but the underground network that makes your life work. In this psalm, let us examine the underground of your life, the part that God looks at.

## 1. WHAT IS IT TO REGARD "SIN IN THE HEART"?

If I know there is something in my life that should not be there, and if I continue to nourish it, or practice it, then I am regarding iniquity in my heart.

Probably all of us have seen an apple with a worm hole in it. A good question is, "Did the worm begin to bore the hole in the apple from the inside or the outside?" Scientists say that the worm often begins on the inside. In fact, they tell us that the egg was laid on the blossom and was hatched in the heart of the apple. Then later it bored out to the surface.

That is the nature of evil in a human life. It begins within the heart and works itself out. Never forget what the Scripture says about that: "Out of the heart proceed evil thoughts, murders, adulteries, fornications, thefts, false witness, blasphemies" (Matt. 15:19).

What is it to regard sin in the heart? It is to knowingly—openly or secretly—engage in evil. When we regard sin in our lives, we entertain the desire for sin, even though circumstances restrain our actions. It is to reflect upon past evil with pleasure rather than with sorrow. It is to look upon the sin of others with approval. It is to know something is wrong, yet to neglect or refuse to correct it.

Hebrews 12:1 is helpful in this matter. The writer says:

> Therefore we also, since we are surrounded by so
> great a cloud of witnesses, let us lay aside every
> weight, and the sin which so easily ensnares us, and
> let us run with endurance the race that is set before
> us.

That little phrase "the sin which so easily ensnares us" is interesting. What is it in your life that so easily ensnares you? For Eve in Genesis, her area of vulnerability appeared to be pride. For Achan, it was covetousness, clothing, and wealth. For David, it appeared to be lust. For Peter, it seemed to be presumption and self-confidence.

Do you know your area of weakness? If not, be assured that Satan does. He knows my address and he knows yours. And you may be sure he will visit you at your point of weakness.

## 2. WHAT DOES SIN IN THE HEART DO TO YOU?

Consider Psalm 66:18, "If I regard iniquity in my heart, the Lord will not hear." Sin stops up the ears of God so that He does not hear our prayers.

We are told that Mt. Vesuvius sends forth a cloud of smoke by day and a red glow of the fires that burn within by night. Only occasionally is there an explosion of internal fire and gases. Then destruction results from the molten liquid within.

So it is with people. All appears well externally. Then there comes a day when the hidden explodes—unless you have dealt with it.

What damage does sin do in the life of a professing Christian?

1. *Sin divides.* I know of only one thing that can prevent communication with God, and that is sin. Sin is a wall of separation between man and God. It grieves the Holy Spirit and makes our prayers nothing more than empty words.

Isaiah 59:2 tells us:

But your iniquities have separated
    you from your God;
And your sins have hidden
    His face from you,
So that He will not hear.

Amos 3:3 asks, "Can two walk together, unless they are agreed?" The answer is no. Sin destroys oneness. It divides.

2. *Sin dulls.* Samson, in the Book of Judges, toyed with evil until a moral paralysis took hold of him, and he did not know when the Lord left him. Sin has a dulling effect. At first you casually walk in the counsel of the ungodly. Then you stand in the way of sinners. Eventually you pull up a chair and sit down in the seat of the scorners (Ps. 1:1).

Edmund Burke, in one of his speeches on English politics, described the decline of character in a civil statesman:

> The instances are exceedingly rare of men immedi-
> ately passing over a clearly marked line from virtue
> into declared vice. There are middle tints and shades
> between the two extremes; there is something uncer-
> tain on the confines of the two empires which they
> must pass through, and which renders the change
> easy and imperceptible.

Yes, sin dopes and dulls until you no longer care who knows about your condition.

3. *Sin drains.* A man in the country watched an American eagle mount into the sky upon its mighty wings. It was a magnificent sight; but soon it appeared that something was wrong. The king of birds did not continue to rise in the sky with the same power and speed. At first his flight was hampered and then stopped until at last it plunged to the ground.

The man, upon examining the bird, found the eagle was dead. Searching more closely, he observed that a small weasel had dug its claws into the abdomen of the splendid bird. It had soared upward with the eagle into the sky and had drained its life-blood while the eagle tried to escape.

Sin works like that. It drains your spiritual life until you are weak and lifeless. Sin begins so very small, but is huge with future consequences.

4. *Sin defeats.* The Old Testament Book of Joshua describes Israel's marvelous victory at the city of Jericho. Israel triumphed, and God was greatly honored. But Joshua 7 records a sad defeat at Ai. Why did Israel experience defeat?

Joshua 7:11 gives the answer: "Israel has sinned." Achan said, "I saw . . . I coveted . . . and took" (7:21). The sin of one man brought defeat to the entire nation.

This speaks to the corporate oneness of God's people. We *are* our brother's keeper! We do not live just for ourselves. No person is an island. Sin causes defeat.

5. *Sin drives us out from God's presence.* Cain killed his brother and went out from the presence of the Lord. Jacob deceived Esau and fled to a strange land. The prodigal son rebelled against his father and went out into a far country. Peter denied his Lord and went out and wept bitterly. Judas betrayed his Master and went out and hanged himself. It is the nature of sin to drive us out—that is the result of sin in the life. Sin can never draw us close to God; it only forces us further and further away.

6. *Sin closes the ears of God.* Again, Psalm 66:18 says, "The Lord will not hear." Proverbs 28:9 tells us, "One who turns away his ear from hearing the Law, even his prayer shall be an abomination." God said to Judah in Isaiah 1:15, "When you spread out your hands, I will hide My eyes from you; even though you make many prayers I will not hear. Your hands are full of blood." God will not listen to the one who harbors sin in his life!

Sin creates a vicious cycle. It condemns the unbelief and sin in a believer's life. It renders him powerless and ineffective.

We must search ourselves and ask of ourselves these questions:

1. Are we honest? Do we give 16 ounces to the pound? Do we have a double standard?
2. Do we have a forgiving spirit? Do we hang on to grudges?
3. Have we robbed God of time, tithe, or talent? Do we seek *first* the kingdom of God?
4. Do we love our neighbor as ourselves?
5. Are we afflicted with spiritual pride?
6. Are we actively doing God's will?

Is something robbing you of God's power? Is there something in your life that separates you from Him?

### 3. THE CURE TO INIQUITY IN THE HEART
While Scripture describes for us the tragic effects of sin, it also provides a remedy for the problem.

1. *Recognize your situation.* Face each obstacle the best you know how. Matthew 5:23-24 tells us:

> Therefore if you bring your gift to the altar, and there remember that your brother has something against you, leave your gift there before the altar, and go your way. First be reconciled to your brother, and then come and offer your gift.

It is a mistake to sit at home, waiting for people to come to you. Write that letter today. Say, "I'm sorry; I'm wrong." Job in the Old Testament lost his health, wealth, and the lives of his children. He was falsely accused by his friends. But the turning point in his situation came when he prayed for his miserable accusers. "And the Lord restored Job's losses when he prayed for his friends. Indeed the Lord gave Job twice as much as he had before" (Job 42:10).

2. *Confess your sin.* David prayed:

> Wash me thoroughly from my iniquity,
> And cleanse me from my sin.
> For I acknowledge my transgressions,
> And my sin is ever before me . . . .
> Wash me, and I shall be whiter than snow . . . .
> Restore to me the joy of Your
>     salvation (Ps. 51:2-3, 7, 12).

To confess is to recognize sin for what it is and call it what God calls it. By doing so, He then washes that sin from us. The Apostle John says in 1 John 1:9, "If we confess our sins, He is faithful and just to forgive us our sins and to cleanse us from all unrighteousness."

3. *Set aside evil actions.* Resolve to put on the Lord Jesus Christ and put off the works of the flesh.

You might ask, "How can I keep from sin?" Let me suggest that you maintain a quiet time. Practice self-examination. The poet has written, "Though my own eyes accuse me not of walking in false disguise, I beg the trial of Thine eyes."

Fill your life with the Bible. Here are two verses from Psalm 119:

> How can a young man cleanse his way?
> By taking heed according to Your Word. . . .
> Your Word I have hidden in my heart,
> That I might not sin against You (vv. 9, 11).

D.L. Moody said, "The Bible will keep you from sin, or sin will keep you from the Bible."

Consider the Cross. Realize that sin placed every scourge on Jesus' back. Sin placed the crown of thorns on Jesus' brow. Sin drove the nails into Jesus' hands and feet. Sin thrust the spear into His side. Remember the truth of Horatio Spafford's "It Is

Well with My Soul":

> My sin—oh, the bliss of this glorious thought,
> My sin—not in part, but the whole,
> Is nailed to the cross and I bear it no more,
> Praise the Lord, praise the Lord, O my soul!

What is the cure for sin in the life? (1) Recognize your spiritual condition; (2) confess your failure and sin; and (3) resolve that Jesus Christ will have first place in your life. These three steps will open your life to God's life. These steps will restore the underground city and bring light, strength, and power to the visible city.

## REMEMBER

If I know there is something in my life that should not be there, and if I continue to nourish it, or practice it, then I am regarding iniquity in my heart.

"Let us lay aside every weight, and the sin which so easily ensnares us" (Heb. 12:1).

Satan knows my address and he knows yours. And you may be sure he will visit you at your point of weakness.

"If I regard iniquity in my heart, the Lord will not hear me" (Ps. 66:18).

Sin begins so very small but is huge with future consequences.

Sin can never draw us closer to God; it only forces us further and further away from Him.

"The Bible will keep you from sin, or sin will keep you from the Bible."—D.L. Moody

# CHAPTER TWELVE

# A CALL TO WORSHIP

## PSALM 100

One evening during World War II a group of French believers gathered in a chapel for a vesper service in northeastern France. While the worshipers were reciting the Scriptures, a bomb ripped through the roof and exploded in the nave of the chapel. For a few moments, dust and smoke filled the chapel. But when the dust settled and the smoke disappeared, the people were still there, reciting from the Bible.

They had not run for cover, but rather, in the midst of great trouble, they continued in worship. These believers knew a lot about the importance of worship.

What is worship? J.I. Packer gives this definition: "It is the deliberate lifting of one's eyes from man and his mistakes to contemplate God and His glory." In other words, when we worship, we think of the worthiness of God.

The word *worship* comes from the Anglo-Saxon word *worthship*. In the Middle Ages, the royalty of Europe were sometimes addressed as "your worship" or "your worthship." It was recognized that their sovereignty and worth was God-given—derived from God alone, who is worthy.

The intention of worship in the Bible is to declare the saving power of God and to make that power a reality in our lives. We worship because of who God is and what He has done. Worship, then, is the highest activity we can engage in. When we glorify God, we proclaim His worth. We worship.

In Psalm 100 we find a well-known call to worship. It has been recited by Jews and Christians throughout the centuries. Its concepts deserve our study. If we listen closely to Psalm 100, we will see three important ideas about worship: why we worship; whom we worship; and how we worship.

## 1. WHY WE WORSHIP

To the modern mind, worship might seem impractical, even an imposition. It means getting up on Sunday morning—the one day designed to sleep in. It means missing all the national news programs. It usually means getting the family all dressed up. What could be more impractical than that? What good reason would cause us to go to this bother just to worship God? Some people see it as an outmoded rite left from a prescientific age. Some Christians leave worship to the liturgically minded churches, preferring cozy fellowship groups instead.

Psalm 100 answers the question of why we worship. Verse 3 reads, "Know that the Lord, He is God; it is He who has made us, and not we ourselves." We worship because the Lord Himself is God.

All people worship in some form or another. Some men worship themselves—they bow to their own desires and live according to their own wishes. Others worship money. Still others worship science, pinning all their hopes on the progress science will bring as it changes our world. The Bible tells us that whatever takes the place of God in our lives becomes an object of worship.

The psalmist says that "the Lord is God." By that he means

that Jehovah of Israel alone is the supreme Deity of the world. Consider what that means: There is no one more worthy of our worship than this God. No one else compares to Him.

Psalm 100:3 continues: "It is He who has made us, and not we ourselves." In other words, we are dependents. The IRS might not recognize you as a dependent, but in God's eyes you are.

We talk a lot about the "self-made man"—the hero of the American dream. But face it—Psalm 100 says, "It is [God] who has made us, and not we ourselves."

At best we are weak, feeble creatures. One out of every three Americans gets cancer. Doctors, scientists, and even Presidents get cancer. And when they find a cure for cancer, something else will come along. Death is inescapable. We are dependent!

Though we strive for greater security, we will always be thrown back on the reality of our human finiteness. We are dependent. When we fail to recognize our dependence upon God, we declare our independence from God. This is self-worship or pride. And there is no more pathetic sight than a man worshiping himself.

## 2. WHOM DO WE WORSHIP?

We learn more about why we should worship by noticing whom we worship. Whom do we worship? Verse 3 makes this clear: "Know that the Lord, He is God." This knowledge is not merely factual knowledge. It is a practical, experiential, and moral knowledge. We are to become intimately acquainted with the Lord God.

So much in this jet age attempts to keep us from really knowing God. When both husband and wife work, schedules become hectic. Wives lose the privilege they once had of being spared from the rat race. Work and career become the family's all-consuming activity, leaving little time for cultivating a knowledge of God.

When we are too busy to worship God, we are *too busy*. Our

work becomes an idol. Elsewhere in the Psalms, God speaks in the clamor of human activity with the words, "Be still, and know that I am God" (46:10).

Who speaks? The Lord does. The title *Lord* stands for the name by which God revealed Himself to Israel, "Jehovah." God said to Moses in Exodus 6:3: " 'I appeared to Abraham, to Isaac, and to Jacob, as God Almighty, but by My name, Lord, I was not known to them.' "

"Jehovah" was the sacred personal name of God specially revealed to Moses. It became associated with God's redeeming activity. Jehovah was a delivering God who saved His people out of Egypt. He was to be known and worshiped as Saviour.

Not only is the Lord God, He is the Creator. He not only created the world, but He made us. He is the all-powerful God.

But this Jehovah God is also a loving, caring Shepherd. He guides, sustains, and provides for us. He cares for you, like no one else does.

What does this mean to us? The New Testament tells us that we have received a better revelation than Moses. We have the revelation of Jesus. In Jesus, we have a more complete look at God. He encourages us to cast all our cares upon Him, because He cares for us.

Psalm 100:5 reads: "For the Lord is good; His mercy is everlasting, and His truth endures to all generations." We worship an omnipotent God, a caring Shepherd who is good, merciful, and faithful.

## 3. HOW WE WORSHIP

Knowing something of why we worship and whom we worship, we must say something about the way we worship.

Psalm 100 is not an exhaustive guide to worship. It is only "a call to worship." But as a call, it provides instruction.

The predominant theme of Psalm 100 is the joy of worship. A book by that title was published some years ago. Other books out include *The Joy of Cooking, The Joy of Sex,* and even *The Joy of Electronics.* Surely, these are all trivial pursuits when compared to "The Joy of Worship."

The Jews have received bad press regarding their worship. When we think of Old Testament worship, we first think of the somber, elaborate rituals Israel had. We forget the joy. Psalm 100 is a psalm of joyful worship. It tells us to "make a joyful shout to the Lord" (v. 1). The Knox translation puts it this way, "Let the whole earth keep holiday in God's honor."

Psalm 100 was probably a favorite psalm in Israel's corporate worship. Israel probably used it in ceremonial processions to the temple. It says, "Come before His presence with singing" (v. 2). And, "Enter into His gates with thanksgiving, and into His courts with praise" (v. 4). Here Israel is celebrating! It is a holiday! We often forget that Israel was commanded to gather three times a year to celebrate the goodness of God. Israel had something to celebrate—the goodness of their Creator and Redeemer. These were joyous times.

Our world also tries to celebrate, but emptiness characterizes their celebrations. College students anxiously anticipate the weekend and its parties. The business crowd has its "happy hour" and "cocktail party," celebrating the end of work—and the end of sobriety!

Israel had a much higher view both of work and celebration. They really had something to shout about. People came from all over the country for these majestic festivals.

Psalm 100 mentions two aspects of their worship: singing and thanksgiving. Verse 4 reads: "Enter into His gates with thanksgiving, and into His courts with praise."

First, the people sang. They sang praises to God. They sang as a congregation at their festivals. They sang in family gatherings. They sang privately during the workweek. In each case, the intention of their song was to praise God for their circumstances. They desired to let the glory of God permeate the details of daily living.

As believers in Jesus Christ, we have the same joy. For that reason Paul admonished the believers at Ephesus to speak "to one another in psalms and hymns and spiritual songs, singing and making melody in your heart to the Lord" (Eph. 5:19).

The Book of Psalms serves as a hymnbook for the godly, a songbook for the soul. In the early centuries of the church, seminary students were often required to memorize all 150 psalms!

When Jerome, the early church father, visited Bethlehem in the fourth century, he was struck by the way psalm singing was universal in the Holy Land. He wrote home, saying:

> Wherever you turn, the laborer at the plow says "Alleluia," the toiling reaper (whiles away) his work with psalms; the vinedresser as he prunes the vine with his curved pruning hook sings something of David's. These are the songs of this province.

Yes, for Christians too, songs of praise should punctuate our lives at home, at work, at play. Songs are an essential part of our worship.

A second aspect of Israel's worship was thanksgiving. Verse 4 instructs, "Enter into His gates with thanksgiving." Notice, worship involves not taking, but giving. When you ask the average churchgoer why he attends church, he usually says "to get fed." But worship is giving back to God.

Synonymous with worship is the word *serve*. Thus, "Serve the Lord with gladness" (v. 2) can be paraphrased, "Worship the Lord with gladness." At worship we minister to the Lord. And what more marvelous way to minister to the Lord than by giving thanks to Him.

Our pilgrim fathers were a thankful people. Three years after they settled in at Plymouth in Massachusetts, Governor Bradford made a thanksgiving proclamation. He said that God had blessed them that year with an abundant harvest of Indian corn, wheat, peas, beans, squash, and other garden vegetables.

God had made the forest to abound with game and the sea with fish and clams. Bradford said that God had protected them and granted them freedom to worship Him. So in 1621, he gathered with his fellow pilgrims to hear his pastor thank God for all their blessings.

How much more should those who know forgiveness through the blood of Christ offer continual thanks to God.

These two aspects of worship, singing and thanksgiving, are essential to each of us.

True worship requires an inner preparation of the heart. A Puritan writer puts it this way: "If thou wouldst have thy heart with God on the Saturday night, thou shouldest find it with Him in the Lord's Day morning." In other words, if you expect to worship God from your heart on Sunday, your heart should be tuned on Saturday night.

Yes, true worship demands heart preparation. Israel was prepared to worship in Psalm 100. Good celebrations require detailed preparation. The people who joined in the procession to the temple were prepared with thanksgiving in their hearts and a song on their lips.

I heard about a man who dreamed that he was escorted into a church by an angel. There was something strange about the service. The organist moved his fingers over the keys, but no music could be heard. As the congregation sang, their lips moved, but not a sound was heard. "What does this mean?" asked the dreamer.

The angel replied, "You hear nothing because they worship just as God sees it. The people are not putting their hearts into the service—only their lips—and therefore God hears nothing."

Jesus spoke about the empty worship of the scribes and Pharisees, " 'These people draw near to Me with their mouth, and honor Me with their lips, but their heart is far from Me' " (Matt. 15:8).

Will you respond with the psalmist in thanksgiving and great praise for His mercy, salvation, and faithfulness?

The Lord wants the worship of our hearts. Have you given Him this service? Will you look to Jesus as your Leader in worship? Consider how He saves His people from sin. Know that He is alive and present with His people. He wants to teach us, to guide us, to comfort us. He is present with all His power and in all His offices as Prophet, Priest, and King.

## REMEMBER

The intention of worship in the Bible is to declare the saving power of God and to make that power a reality in our lives.

When we fail to recognize our dependence upon God, we declare our independence from God.

When we are too busy to worship God, we are too busy.

The Book of Psalms serves as a hymnbook for the godly, a songbook for the soul.

Worship involves not taking, but giving.

True worship requires an inner preparation of the heart.

# CHAPTER THIRTEEN

# BLESSING IS A TWO-WAY STREET

## PSALM 103

T he Bible often makes use of the word *bless*. Unfortunately, the modern use of the word has limited it so that we fail to recognize its greatness. Somehow, the word has been sidelined, except for its use in the mealtime prayer or the empty response to a sneeze.

When David used the word *bless*, he used it with dignity. In Psalm 103 he breaks out into praise: "Bless the Lord, O my soul; and all that is within me, bless His holy name!" (Ps. 103:1)

Blessing is a two-way street. Only because God blessed us by creating us and saving us can we respond by blessing Him. Consider (1) the meaning of blessing, (2) the call to bless, and (3) the reasons to bless.

## 1. THE MEANING OF BLESSING

The idea of blessing in the Old Testament first occurs in Genesis 1:22. After the account of the fourth day of Creation, when God made the animal world, we read: "God blessed them, saying, 'Be fruitful and multiply.' " Then on the fifth day, when God had made man, verse 28 says, "God blessed them, and God said to them, 'Be fruitful and multiply; fill the earth and subdue it.' "

Up to this point, blessing was only a one-way street. God gave, gave, and gave. Man received. We never read that Adam or Eve blessed the Lord. We hear only of their offenses.

Not until Genesis 9, after the account of the Flood, does blessing become more than a one-way street. In Genesis 9:1, we read, "God blessed Noah and his sons." Then finally, in verse 26 of chapter 9 Noah said, "Blessed be the Lord."

The Old Testament word *bless* carries two shades of meaning: First, it means "to endow with beneficial power," and second, "to worship or praise." Obviously we cannot give God beneficial power, but we can respond to God's blessing with a response of adoration. We can say with David: "Bless the Lord, O my soul; and all that is within me, bless His holy name!" (Ps. 103:1)

Later the psalmist calls all creation to join in praising God: "Bless the Lord, all you His hosts" (v. 21); and, "Bless the Lord, all His works" (v. 22). What a privilege to bless God in praise and worship.

## 2. THE CALL TO BLESS

Verses 1-2 and 20-22 call us to bless God. The call to bless is a call to worship with praise.

Who is to bless God? It might surprise you, but the call to bless God rings throughout the entire universe.

First, David calls himself to worship. He speaks to himself. "Bless the Lord, O my soul; and all that is within me." He calls to his own soul. He calls for his entire being to bless God.

As Christians, sometimes we must call ourselves out of our own spiritual slumber. The Welsh preacher Martin Lloyd-Jones said that of all people, Christians should talk to themselves. Talking to oneself signifies, not mental abnormality, but mental health. "The Scriptures," Lloyd-Jones said, "teach us how to talk to ourselves." We must remind ourselves who we are and what our calling is. When lethargy or pride threatens to control us, we must speak up and say no to laziness, no to pride. When tempted to sink into a spiritual stupor, we must rouse ourselves like the psalmist and say, "Bless the Lord, O my soul!"

But the most beautiful kind of praise comes in the form of corporate praise—the praise of God's gathered assembly. By the end of Psalm 103, David can no longer stand to sing alone, so he calls out to the angels, God's servants:

> Bless the Lord, you His angels,
> Who excel in strength, who do His word,
> Heeding the voice of His word (v. 20).

Then David shouts to all the heavenly creatures:

> Bless the Lord, all you His hosts,
> You ministers of His, who do His pleasure (v. 21).

Next David personifies creation in verse 22 and invites all of God's handiwork to join the chorus:

> Bless the Lord, all His works,
> In all places of His dominion.

During World War II a cynical English soldier found himself stationed in a French village. Nothing pleased him more than mocking the old village pastor. One morning, as he walked by the church, he saw a handful of parishioners leaving the service.

"Good morning, Pastor," he said. "Not very many at church this morning."

"No, my son, you're wrong," replied the pastor. "Thousands and thousands and tens of thousands were in the church."

That pastor grasped something that the soldier was too blind to see—the corporate, universal dimension of God's great family.

The Book of Common Prayer includes a prayer called the "Te Deum," Latin for "we praise Thee." This amazing prayer recognizes the glory of God. It begins: "We praise Thee, O God; we acknowledge Thee to be Lord."

Then it goes on to say how the earth also praises God, as do the angels and the cherubim and seraphim. Surely this is an echo of Psalm 103.

The prayer continues:

> The glorious company of the apostles praise Thee.
> The goodly fellowship of the prophets praise Thee.
> The noble army of martyrs praise Thee.
> The whole church throughout all the world doth
> acknowledge Thee.

How limited and provincial our praise sometimes becomes! How cloistered our worship services. We forget that worship is an eternal song sung through the centuries. We forget too that when our congregations bless God on Sunday mornings, something marvelous happens: we join a chorus of adoration as it is sung in heaven!

Hymnwriter Henry Lyte states it beautifully in "Praise, My Soul, the King of Heaven":

> Angels, help us to adore Him,
>     Ye behold Him face to face;
> Sun and moon, bow down before Him;
>     Dwellers all in time and space,
> Alleluia! Alleluia!
>     Praise with us the God of grace!

The Doxology that we often sing so mechanically says it so well:

Praise God from whom all blessings flow,
Praise Him all creatures here below,
Praise Him above ye heavenly hosts,
Praise Father, Son, and Holy Ghost.

## 3. REASONS TO BLESS

The call to worship God with praise gives only one meaning to the word *bless*. But consider a second meaning. To discover it, we must understand the reasons why the psalmist blesses God. He gives us two reasons: (1) He blesses God for His benefits—for what God confers on His creatures; and (2) he also blesses Him for His person—for what God is in Himself.

First let us ask what benefits David has in mind. Verse 2 says, "Bless the Lord, O my soul, and forget not all His benefits." Then he lists these benefits in verses 3-5. David begins with a series of statements:

Who forgives all your iniquities,
Who heals all your diseases,
Who redeems your life from destruction,
Who crowns you with loving-kindness
    and tender mercies,
Who satisfies your mouth with good things.

Some commentators believe that David was ill at this point, but on his way to recovery. While recovering, he reflected with grateful wonder on the delivering power of God. He concludes that a total recovery calls for total praise. So he blesses God for all His benefits.

Whatever the psalmist's immediate situation, he speaks to life's most pressing issues—forgiveness, sickness, death, long life, and prosperity. In verses 6 and 7, he adds injustice and ignorance to the list.

The psalmist's words come from personal experience. Essentially he says, "I was guilty of wrongdoing. The only release I found was in God's forgiveness. I was plagued with diseases. The ultimate healer of my illnesses is the Omnipotent God. I was threatened by death. The only escape I found was in His eternal salvation."

The psalmist refers to the very things we struggle with on a daily basis. He looks to the Lord for deliverance because only in Him can we experience complete freedom. It begins in this life, but its results go on into eternity.

Consider pardon, for instance. David says in verses 10-12:

> He has not dealt with us according to our sins,
> Nor punished us according to our iniquities.
> For as the heavens are high above the earth,
> So great is His mercy toward those who fear Him;
> As far as the east is from the west,
> So far has He removed our transgressions from us.

He speaks of the grace of an unfathomable forgiveness. None of us deserve to get off free. In a moral universe, someone must pay. Yet that burden has been removed for David. And it can be lifted from you too, if you trust in God's final answer for sin—the Lord Jesus Christ. Have you experienced God's forgiveness? To all who receive Jesus Christ, our sins have been removed—as far as the east is from the west!

Why should we bless God? Because He has poured out so many benefits on all of creation and countless more on those who have believed in Him.

David tells us, "Forget none of His benefits." In other words, keep track of His blessings in your life. The memory becomes a lethal spiritual weapon. When our feelings get low, and we no longer sense the presence of God, we can remind ourselves of God's past blessing, not only to ourselves, but on our extended family and to His church. We keep a list of these.

I once wrote down a brief account of my grandparents' conversion. I recorded the special healing from sickness in my own life. I recall the conversion of my children, and the way the Lord brought them their wives. I bring to mind His pardon for my sins and those moments when I sensed His presence so very real and near.

One of the key words in the Old Testament Law is "remember." The Scriptures call Israel to remember its release from captivity in Egypt. When Israel remembered, she brought God's loving-kindness to mind. This kept her from becoming spiritually self-complacent.

The psalmist echoes this summons when he calls, "Forget none of His benefits." He calls us to the hardest type of arithmetic to master—that which enables us to count our blessings. This is not an exercise in religious sentimentalism. Rather, it is a choice way to regain perspective on our lives—to credit grace to God's account and not to our own.

I heard about a professional beggar who had the words *thank you* tattooed on the palm of his right hand. These words should be tattooed on the hearts of each of us.

In the first chapter of Ephesians, Paul overflowed with praise when he wrote: "Blessed be the God and Father of our Lord Jesus Christ, who has blessed us with every spiritual blessing in the heavenly places in Christ" (v. 3).

Here Paul uses the twofold meaning of the word *bless*. He speaks of blessing as a two-way street. We bless God because He first blessed us. How did He bless us in Christ? Ephesians 1 goes on to describe this. He says God chose us in Christ (v. 4). He adopted us (v. 5). He redeemed us (v. 7). He forgave us (v. 7). He made His will known to us (v. 9). He sealed us (v. 13). After listing this lavish catalog of blessing, Paul charges the Ephesians to know the hope of their calling. He echoes the psalmist who said, "Forget none of these benefits."

Why should we bless God? Not only because of what He does, but also because of who He is. Verse 1 of Psalm 103 says, "Bless His holy name."

Did you know that God's name stands for His entire personality? When we bless His name we bless the sum of His attributes.

Psalm 103 uses only one name for God, His special revealed name—Jehovah ("the Lord"). This is God's personal name, the name He revealed to Moses. God entrusted Israel with that name as a special revelation.

I once heard of a middle-aged woman who believed she needed a facelift to improve her appearance. At the same time she experienced heart problems. The doctors told her they could cure the problem with extensive surgery, or control it with medication. She decided her next operation would be the best facelift money could buy. She invested more care in changing her face than her heart. That, my friend, is a sad commentary on her values. All too often we apply the medication to the wrong places.

The promise in Psalm 103 follows in verses 17 and 18:

> But the mercy of the Lord is from
>     everlasting to everlasting
> On those who fear Him,
> And His righteousness to children's children,
> To such as keep His covenant,
> And to those who remember His
>     commandments to do them.

Did you catch that? If God's loving-kindness is everlasting, and if He directs it at those who fear Him, then *we* can have eternal life! We can escape the ultimate clutches of death and decay. These verses tell us that, though we are finite and flawed, we are also favored. God's infinite love can preserve our souls. It is a gift.

Sin flawed us and made us finite. But the good news of the Gospel tells us that God favors us. Will you open your life to Jesus Christ and commit yourself to Him fully?

Do you know the blessing of abundant life? Have you accepted God's gracious pardon in Jesus Christ? When you do, blessing becomes a superhighway where the traffic of God's gifts is abundant! If you have, you can say with the psalmist,

> Bless the Lord, O my soul;
> And all that is within me,
>   bless His holy name!

## REMEMBER

Blessing is a two-way street. Only because God blessed us by creating us and saving us can we respond by blessing Him.

The call to bless God rings throughout the entire universe. "The Scriptures teach us how to talk to ourselves."—Martin Lloyd-Jones

Keep track of His blessings in your life. The memory becomes a lethal spiritual weapon.

When we bless God's name, we bless the sum of His attributes.

# CHAPTER FOURTEEN

# THE REUNION OF THE REDEEMED

## PSALM 107

**M**any unforgettable reunions occurred at the close of World War II. Surviving soldiers returned to anxious families. Refugees returned to see what was left of their homes. Captives returned from prison camps, wondering if loved ones escaped death.

Reunions are fascinating. Most of those attending a reunion have stories to tell. School reunions, military reunions, and even family reunions bring endless accounts and reaccountings of lost years. Some are sad. Some are glad.

Psalm 107 is a Hebrew song about the reunion of exiles from captivity. These Jewish captives endured much together. They experienced oppression at the hands of the Babylonians. They served as slaves to harsh Gentile rulers. The heathen nations destroyed their beloved temple. Their captors proclaimed the special Jewish holidays illegal. But then, they began to hope again.

Ezekiel and other prophets said that some of them would return to Palestine. That hope became more believable as the

Babylonian Empire began to decline and Cyrus of Persia defeated the Babylonians. In 538 B.C., King Cyrus issued a decree allowing all the captive Jews to return to Palestine and resume their worship. Can you picture that reunion? Just imagine the experiences they had to share! Psalm 107:1-3 tells us about it:

> Oh, give thanks to the Lord,
>     for He is good!
> For His mercy endures forever.
> Let the redeemed of the Lord say so,
> Whom He has redeemed from the hand
>     of the enemy.
> And gathered out of the lands,
> From the east and from the west.
> From the north and from the south.

If these Hebrew people understood one thing, they knew that their prayers to God during their captivity had been heard. God answered their prayers and opened the way for them to return home. This was the reunion of the redeemed.

This psalm tells four exile stories, the stories of a lost people, a captive people, a sick people, and a storm-tossed people. Each story attests to the helplessness of man in his troubles, and the great saving power of God. They praise a God who has delivered His people in both ordinary and extraordinary circumstances.

## 1. A LOST PEOPLE

At the outset this psalm relates the story of a lost people (vv. 4-9). It tells of travelers wandering in a desert, unable to find their way to a city. To make matters worse, their supplies have dwindled to nothing. Verse 5 says, "Hungry and thirsty, their soul fainted in them." In desperation they prayed: "Then they cried out to the Lord in their trouble, and He delivered them out of their distresses" (v. 6). Then it tells how God heard and delivered them from their agony. "And He led them forth by the right way, that they might go to a city for habitation" (v. 7).

The first story ends with an exhortation to those who were delivered: "Oh, that men would give thanks to the Lord for His goodness, and for His wonderful works to the children of men!" (v. 8)

The pattern here is plain. The people found themselves in a desperate situation. Those involved cried out to God, and in mercy God delivered them.

Psalm 107 pictures lost travelers. Possibly it finds its setting on the long journey from Babylon to Palestine. It also portrays the plight of the nation lost in exile. They had ignored God's roadmap and were perishing, scattered among the nations.

It is not by accident that Jesus tells in Matthew 18 of the shepherd seeking the lost sheep that went astray. Jesus said, "Does he not leave the ninety-nine and go to the mountains to seek the one that is straying?" (v. 12) Jesus saw His ministry in this same way. People, separate from God, are lost and in trouble. Jesus said that the "Son of Man has come to seek and to save that which was lost" (v. 11).

This first story indicates that God heard the cry of a lost people and saved them out of their troubles. He gave them direction to come home.

## 2. A CAPTIVE PEOPLE

A second story told by the returned exiles involves a group of captives. They were imprisoned. Verse 10 describes them: "Those who sat in darkness and in the shadow of death, bound in affliction and irons." Verse 12 characterizes the situation as oppressive: "They fell down, and there was none to help."

In desperation they cried out to the Lord. Verse 13 tells us that "He saved them out of their distresses." God broke their chains. He shattered the brass prison gates. He cut the iron bars in pieces.

In response to such a marvelous display, the psalmist said, "Oh, that men would give thanks to the Lord for His goodness, and for His wonderful works to the children of men!" (v. 15)

The vivid details tell us that this was someone's real experience. But more than being an isolated incident, this represents the fate of Israel in Babylon. They experienced the dungeon of exile—crushed and oppressed. Yet, as happened when they were in bondage in Egypt, God heard their cry and delivered them from captivity.

This second story of Psalm 107 also tells us the results of ignoring God's Word. Verse 11 says that "they rebelled against the words of God, and despised the counsel of the Most High."

Whenever anyone declares his freedom from God, he binds himself to something else. He trades off a captivity of one sort or the other. Everyone is bound to something. If not God, then we are bound to something else—possibly ourselves.

Our God is in the business of freeing captives. He delivered Joseph in the Old Testament. He miraculously freed Peter from jail. He did the same for Paul and Silas, and He frees men and women today.

Jesus' primary ministry is to free people from sin. He frees us to become His loving servants. Do you know that freedom? Have you experienced His saving power? If so, as verse 2 says, "Let the redeemed of the Lord say so." To be silent is sinful.

### 3. A SICK PEOPLE

Psalm 107 portrays a third incident about a sick people. Verses 17-22 say that they were afflicted. They were so ill they would not eat. Their sickness brought them to the verge of death. Then they cried to God for help. Verses 19 and 20 say, "Then they cried out to the Lord in their trouble, and He saved them out of their distresses. He sent His word and healed them."

Notice the similarities between Israel then and us today. Their bodies decayed as do ours. This story tells us of those who in the common sicknesses cried out to God, and He miraculously made them whole.

But another level of truth lies hidden here, because these "sick people" stand for the Hebrew children in exile. They rebelled before God and God caused them to lose their homeland. Their disease was a cancer of the soul. Their iniquities brought them afflictions. As such, their illness could be healed only by the Word of God.

Often Jesus compassionately healed the sick during His earthly ministry. He still can, and often does. Of course, each of us will eventually get sick. Sometimes in response to faith God heals us. Often God uses proper care, rest, and medicine. Sometimes God heals in death, because death releases us from a disease-ridden body. Then He raises us to eternal life and a resurrection body.

## 4. A STORM-TOSSED PEOPLE

The fourth picture of Israel and of ourselves comes in Psalm 107:23-32. It tells of a people caught in a storm at sea. The descriptions are vivid. Those facing the storm experienced dangerous winds. The waves grew large. Verse 26 says that the rising swells of the water appeared to raise the boat to the heavens, and then sink it to the depths. The people were petrified. Their souls melted in misery.

> They reel to and fro,
>     and stagger like a drunken man,
> And are at their wits' end.
> Then they cry out to the Lord in their trouble,
> And He brings them out of their distresses.
> He calms the storm,
> So that its waves are still (vv. 27-29).

And then verse 30 reads:

> Then they are glad because they are quiet;

123

So He guides them to their desired haven.

Again the psalmist gratefully responds, "Oh, that men would give thanks to the Lord for His goodness, and for His wonderful works to the children of men!" The exile of the Children of Israel paralleled being caught in the storm. The sea of nations swallowed them up. Hope for a future appeared lost.

Yet there is good news for storm-tossed people because God can calm the storm. He can command the nations to quiet down and be at peace.

Twice in Jesus' ministry, we read how He rebuked the wind and the sea. As He calmed the storms then, He can today, if only people will call to Him in the storm. Are you tossed by a storm? It might be a storm of suffering, of doubt, of financial crisis, or of broken relationships. Jesus offers to help you.

Can you imagine these exiles telling accounts of their deliverance? Each one seemed bigger and better. But they make the point that God had redeemed His people from many troubles and they were glad. This was a reunion of the redeemed.

And my friend, God's redeeming activity is not over. Our God is a transforming God. Give Him a difficult situation, and He can change it.

Verses 35-38 tell of God's miraculous ability to change a wilderness into a pool of water. He does this for His children. Ezekiel said that God can take old dry bones and make them live again. This was the hope of the returned exiles. They wanted to live again as a nation. They wanted to be faithful to the Lord. They wanted to start over again.

Is this where you find yourself today? Maybe you are lost in a sea of details. Maybe something has you bound, something from which you wish to be free. Possible fear over a sick body has you paralyzed. Or maybe the storm has brought you to the end of your rope. Stop trying to save yourself. Realize that you are no match for some of your enemies. Someone has said, "When you get to the end of your rope, tie a knot and hang on." Better advice would be, "When you get to the end of your rope, let go and fall into the arms of God."

In every instance of Psalm 107, the exiles despaired of their own efforts. They cried to God. He saved them. He found the lost. He freed the captive. He healed the sick. He calmed the sea. He alone saves.

But you may say, "If God saved Israel like that, why do we need Jesus Christ? Why did God bother to send His Son?"

God gave His Son to provide a *total* salvation. In His death and resurrection, Jesus delivered man not only from his temporary troubles, but from his ultimate enemies—sin and death. Unlike the Exodus or the return from exile, or the sacrifices in the temple, Jesus' accomplishment on the cross could be transferred to every generation until the end of time. In its power, in its scope, and in its duration, it marks the high point of God's salvation to mankind. The writer of Hebrews said that Christ "obtained eternal redemption" (9:12).

So we read Psalm 107, knowing that God has done His ultimate work in Jesus Christ. The New Testament Scripture points to Jesus for our salvation. He is the victorious King who lives and intercedes for us. He is the One who delivers us from all oppression. Jesus is the One of whom John 3:16 says, "For God so loved the world that He gave His only begotten Son, that whoever believes in Him should not perish but have everlasting life."

## REMEMBER

It is not by accident that Jesus tells in Matthew 18 of the shepherd seeking the lost sheep that went astray.

Whenever anyone declares his freedom from God, he binds himself to something else.

"Let the redeemed of the Lord say so." To be silent is sinful.

"Oh, that men would give thanks to the Lord for His goodness, and for His wonderful works to the children of men!"

When you get to the end of your rope, let go and fall into the arms of God.

# CHAPTER FIFTEEN

# THANKSGIVING—PURE AND SIMPLE

## PSALM 136

Some of the most thankful people I have ever met live in modest surroundings. They eat simply, buy no luxuries, and seldom take a trip. Some of them are sick and disabled. But they are obviously thankful. Why? They live in the sunlight of God's love, care, and mercy.

What was the first American Thanksgiving like? For sure they ate no pumpkin pies, watched no football games or parades. And it definitely did not launch a hectic Christmas season.

As early as 1607, colonists on the coast of Maine, after disembarking from their ship, gave thanks to God for a safe trip to the New World. At Jamestown, Virginia in 1619, the settlers set apart an entire day to thank God that their settlement had survived their first year. Those celebrations were not so much feasts as they were fasts. The Pilgrims gave themselves to prayer in gratitude for God's mercy.

Later, the Pilgrims of the Plymouth Colony added a Thanksgiving feast. Our history books record that as the first official Thanksgiving.

# THANKSGIVING—PURE AND SIMPLE

The original Thanksgiving celebrations were just that—thanksgiving, pure and simple. This same thanksgiving lies at the heart of Psalm 136.

> Oh, give thanks to the Lord,
>     for He is good! . . .
> Oh, give thanks to the God of gods! . . .
> Oh, give thanks to the Lord of lords! . . .
> Oh, give thanks to the God of heaven!

The psalm heaps layer upon layer of thanksgiving and then repeats the refrain, "For His mercy endures forever." Some translations, including the *New American Standard Bible*, record it as, "God's loving-kindness is everlasting."

The people probably sang this beautiful psalm in the temple as they worshiped. The soloist would sing a phrase of thanks, and then the congregation would respond with the phrase, "His mercy endures forever!" Imagine the resulting symphony echoing off the temple's marble walls and into the streets of the city.

When you experience the warmth and power of God's love and mercy, thanksgiving becomes a very spontaneous thing.

Psalm 136 suggests at least three reasons for Israel's thankfulness. Those three reasons apply to us as well.

## 1. THANKSGIVING FOR THE WONDER OF GOD'S CREATION

Psalm 136 tells us that they gave thanks to God, and then declares that God "alone does great wonders" (v. 4); "by wisdom made the heavens" (v. 5); "laid out the earth above the waters . . . made great light." (vv. 6-7).

The people of Israel took nothing for granted. Have you ever thanked God for space? For the space you occupy? For the space of our planet and nation? For the space in your home?

In Psalm 136, Israel thanked God for food, shelter, protection, and possessions. They thanked God for light. Theories of nuclear winters remind us how desperately we need light.

Then the psalmist gives thanks to God for time: "The sun to rule by day . . . the moon and stars to rule by night" (vv. 8-9). Time is a divine gift, not a human right. We receive the gift of time at birth. We cannot extend it. We cannot buy more of it. Our supply of time is limited. Time eventually runs out, and we can do absolutely nothing about it. Time is a gift.

As believers in Jesus Christ, we too can give thanks to God for His marvelous creation. The Gospel of John, chapter 1, verses 3-4, reminds us, "All things were made through Him [Jesus], and without Him nothing was made that was made. In Him was life, and the life was the light of men." Give thanks for the wonder of God's creation.

## 2. THANKSGIVING FOR GOD'S SALVATION

Like Creation, God's provision of salvation was to be marveled at, not taken for granted. God is the giver, and we are the receivers. This psalm reminds Israel of God's loving favor. Consider Psalm 136, verses 10-18:

> To Him who struck Egypt in their firstborn . . .
> And brought out Israel from among them . . .
> With a strong hand,
>     and with an outstretched arm . . .
> To Him who divided the Red Sea in two . . .
> And made Israel pass through the midst of it . . .
> But overthrew Pharaoh and his army in
>     the Red Sea . . .
> To Him who led His people through
>     the wilderness . . .
> To Him who struck down great kings . . .
> And slew famous kings.

The Children of Israel were overcome with great thanks to God, first for the wonder of Creation; and secondly, for the

128

wonder of God's salvation.

God marvelously delivered them out of the distresses of Egypt. He took them out from literal slavery. God freed them.

The Bible reminds us that everyone is in "spiritual bondage." In ourselves we are "dead in trespasses and sins." Paul writes, in Ephesians 2:4, "But God, who is rich in mercy, because of His great love . . . made us alive together with Christ (by grace you have been saved)" (Eph. 2:4). Have you experienced God's redeeming love?

The great Roman philosopher Seneca exclaimed at one point in his life, "Oh, that a hand were let down to lift me out of my besetting sin."

My friend, the good news of salvation is this: A hand has been let down. That hand belongs to Jesus. He has the ability to lift you and empower you to do what you could never do in your own strength. Place your hand into His hand, and you will experience the wonder of God's full and free salvation.

Years ago I met Seth Sykes in Glasgow, Scotland. Seth and his wife served as evangelists to Scotland. Realizing the wonder of personal salvation, Seth wrote a simple, yet profound little chorus:

> Thank You, Lord, for saving my soul;
> Thank You, Lord, for making me whole;
> Thank You, Lord, for giving to me
> Thy great salvation, so rich and free.

God's salvation was experienced by the nation Israel in deliverance from Egypt, and also in His victory over nature. God divided the Red Sea in two. He removed the pursuing Egyptians. He brought His people through the wilderness. He parted the waters of the Jordan and helped them cross safely into the Promised Land. With that the Children of Israel affirmed, "His mercy endures forever." And it does.

Can you see the parallel between Israel's redemption and the redemption accomplished by Jesus Christ? Jesus' sacrificial death was for you and me. He is the fulfillment of the Passover Lamb. We can only respond, "Oh, give thanks to the Lord, for He is good! For His mercy endures forever."

## 3. THANKSGIVING FOR THE WONDER OF A HOMELAND

Psalm 136 speaks of a third wonder in verses 16-22. Here the people thank God for the wonder of a homeland—prepared by God for His people. Verses 21-26 read:

> And gave their land as a heritage . . .
> A heritage to Israel His servant. . . .
> Who remembered us in our lowly state . . .
> And rescued us from our enemies . . .
> Who gives food to all flesh. . . .
> Oh, give thanks to the God of heaven!

Like creation and salvation, Israel was not to take for granted a prepared homeland. God had promised to lead them to that homeland. He would help them claim it and keep it.

Do you remember how the Lord guided them? He provided a pillar of cloud by day and a pillar of fire by night. Remember too how He provided for them? He gave them water from a rock, and manna from heaven. Remember how He taught them? He gave them His commandments on Mount Sinai as a guide to prosperous living.

As Israel approached the land, they realized that they themselves had a role to play in God's plan. They were to take the land. They were to do battle with local kings. One of the most formidable foes they faced was the powerful Ammorite nation. That nation included more than sixty fortified cities, all with high walls. These had to be conquered. In the Book of Joshua, we read how God led His people into the land, conquering all the nations there. King after king fell before Israel. The battle belonged to the Lord.

Israel gradually possessed a land with cities which they did not establish, and houses which they did not build, and wells which they did not dig, and orchards which they did not plant. This would be the land they had long dreamed about. This would be the land flowing with milk and honey; a land of rest and safety; a land of peace, prosperity, and worship.

Oh, that Israel had remained true to God's Law. But you know the story. They were not much more successful than Adam and Eve in the Garden. Judges ruled. Then kings ruled. Then came civil war. The nation split. Eventually, the Northern Kingdom grew so corrupt that God gave them over to the Assyrians. The Southern Kingdom followed, falling into the hands of Babylonian rulers. Heathen nations laid homeland in waste. The dream was shattered. Hopes were crushed. The people were deported. The next psalm, Psalm 137, tells of the devastated spirits of God's people when they came to their senses. It says, "By the rivers of Babylon, there we sat down, yea, we wept when we remembered Zion" (Ps. 137:1). How cast down they were!

What then remained for them to wonder at since sin disfigured creation and overturned redemption? What was there left to say? Only one thing: They gave thanks to God—"Oh, give thanks to the Lord, for He is good! His mercy endures forever."

Now in the fullness of time, God sent His Son, Jesus, to gather a remnant from Israel and to extend salvation to the Gentiles. Jesus would pick up the mantle of Moses and lead His people. Instead of the pillar of cloud and fire to guide them, He gave the Living Word to fulfill the Law. Instead of manna and water, Jesus gave Himself, the Living Bread and Water.

To His distraught disciples, Jesus simply said:

> Let not your heart be troubled; you believe in God, believe also in Me. In My Father's house are many mansions; if it were not so, I would have told you. I

**131**

go to prepare a place for you. And if I go and prepare a place for you, I will come again and receive you to Myself; that where I am, there you may be also (John 14:1-3).

Israel was to thank God for the wonder of a homeland. And with the perspective of time and the advent of the Messiah, Christians share in this same marvelous hope. We have the promise of a prepared homeland. But, unlike the Old Testament monarchy, Christ's rule will never be overturned. And, unlike the Old Testament thanksgiving, the praise of His people today can only grow more intense, the volume can only increase.

Psalm 136 is thanksgiving, pure and simple. The people of Israel did not gorge themselves unnecessarily, but rather gave great thanks to God. Our responsibility is to remember in a fresh way this thanksgiving. The wonder of God's creation, the wonder of God's great salvation, and the wonder of a homeland for each child of God. Feast, and give thanks with these three truths in mind.

## REMEMBER

The original Thanksgiving celebrations were just that—thanksgiving, pure and simple.

When you experience the warmth and power of God's love and mercy, thanksgiving becomes a very spontaneous thing.

Time is a divine gift, not a human right.

Jesus has the ability to lift you and empower you to do what you could never do in your own strength.

"Oh, give thanks to the Lord, for He is good! For His mercy endures forever" (Ps. 136:1).

*Praise God on good & bad day-*
*Praise God on 1 day we will all be united*
*÷ into groups I verse & follow it*
*Focus on his love endures forever*
*God's loving kindness*